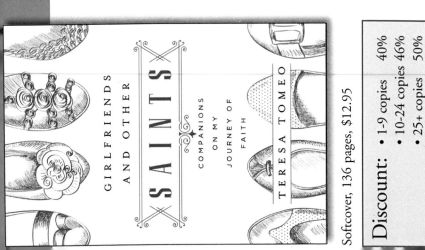

GIRLFRIENDS AND OTHER

SAINTS

COMPANIONS ON MY JOURNEY OF FAITH

GIRLFRIENDS AND OTHER

SAINTS

COMPANIONS
ON MY
JOURNEY OF
FAITH

TERESA TOMEO

the WORD among us® press

Published by The Word Among Us Press
7115 Guilford Drive, Suite 100
Frederick, Maryland 21704
www.wau.org

20 19 18 17 16 1 2 3 4 5

ISBN: 978-1-59325-292-2
eISBN: 978-1-59325-484-1

Cover design by Faceout Studios

Made and printed in the United States of America

Library of Congress Control Number: 2016935628

Contents

Introduction / 7

1. Knocking on Heaven's Door / 13

2. Can We Talk? / 27

3. They Can Hear You Now / 37

4. Every Saint Has a Past, Every Sinner Has a Future / 47

5. The Blessed Mother Is Watching You
—and Listening Too! / 55

6. All Sunshine Makes a Desert / 65

7. Anywhere But There / 75

8. Thoughts Interrupted / 91

9. Walk a Mile in Their Sandals / 101

10. Thank You for Being a Friend / 109

11. Cast Out Your Nets / 117

Conclusion: You're Right Where You Need to Be / 127

Endnotes / 133

"The feeling remains that God is on the journey too."
—St. Teresa of Avila

INTRODUCTION

Friendship . . . is born at the moment when
one man says to another: "What! You too?
I thought that no one but myself . . . "

—C.S. Lewis[1]

A s Christians we are all trying to do our best to love
God and neighbor. But let's not kid ourselves—it's
getting more and more difficult to hold onto our
faith. Right is wrong. Wrong is right. Everything is turning
into a free-for-all. Nowadays, Catholics and other Christians
who are trying to be faithful end up being the ones that nobody
wants to invite to the block party or backyard barbecue. We
can sometimes—and with good reason—feel like the most
unpopular girl at the school dance or the one that nobody
wants to friend on Facebook. We may feel like foreigners in
a very strange land, even among those to whom we thought
we could relate.

But what if we weren't alone? What if we actually had
thousands, yes, thousands upon thousands, of spiritual sup-
porters who were waiting in the wings, standing by, ready
to help us at a moment's—or more specifically, a prayer's—
notice? What would it be like to have on our side a spiritual
giant who had experienced similar trials and tribulations?
What if we could call that saint a friend? Wouldn't that

make us feel much more confident when our feet hit the ground each morning?

Sounds too good to be true, doesn't it? Sounds like something that only happens once in a lifetime or to people who are way more holy than we are. Well, if it happened to me, it can happen to anyone. You might be thinking, "Oh sure. Like some holier-than-thou person whose painting is hanging in the Vatican or some other basilica or cathedral somewhere is actually someone I can relate to and who actually cares about me."

Well, getting to know the saints and learning to reach out to them is part of truly belonging to a loving family. That's what the communion of saints is all about. It means getting the support we need whenever we need it. And if we profess to believe what the Church teaches regarding the saints, then we truly are, as it says in Hebrews 12:1, "surrounded by so great a cloud of witnesses."

In the *Catechism of the Catholic Church*, we're told that we have one heck of a cheering section in heaven.

The witnesses who have preceded us into the kingdom (cf. Hebrews 12:1), especially those whom the Church recognizes as saints, share in the living tradition of prayer by the example of their lives, the transmission of their writings, and their prayer today. They contemplate God, praise him and constantly care for those whom they have left on earth. When they

entered into the joy of their Master, they were "put in charge
of many things" (cf. Matthew 25:21). Their intercession is
their most exalted service to God's plan. We can and should
ask them to intercede for us and for the whole world. (2683)

So why all the "cloudiness" still when it comes to this
great community of witnesses and the role they can and
should play in our lives? Why do so many Catholics, as I
did for years, simply put saints high up on a pedestal (or
place their images and statues on a shelf), merely to be
looked at and admired from afar, when these great men
and women truly want to help us in a very personal way
in our everyday lives?

That's why I wanted to write a different type of book
about the saints. Even though there is no shortage of material written about Catholic saints, I am not aware of many
books that help us see the saints as real friends, fellow sisters or brothers with whom we can share our joys and our
sorrows, and people to whom we can turn when life gets
crazy, as it often does.

No doubt there are books on the lives of a variety of
saints. There are books on praying with the saints. There
are libraries filled with the writings of many well-known
saints such as St. Teresa of Avila, St. Augustine, St. Thomas
Aquinas, and St. Catherine of Siena, just to name a few,
several of whom we'll get to know better over the next

several chapters. But how many books detail modern-day encounters with the saints? And how many books give us practical applications of the Church's teaching to help us bring the saints into our lives in a personal way? What exactly does incorporating the communion of saints in our world really look like? Even if we have favorite patron saints to whom we turn for help with specific issues, do we really consider those saints our friends?

If we would take even just a little bit of time to look at the lives of the saints, we would definitely find a kindred spirit or a soul mate and, no doubt, as in my case, several friends. The saints were real people who often lived very ordinary lives. The difference was that they loved God and their fellow man in extraordinary ways. They were doctors, lawyers, nurses, slaves, rich men, poor men, teachers, fishermen, reformed murderers, former adulterers, soldiers, confessed persecutors of Christians—the list goes on and on. Certainly the communion of saints includes some incredibly holy men and women who lived extremely virtuous lives during their time on planet Earth, but there were just as many whose lives were not so saintly until they discovered Jesus or rediscovered him later in life. Surely among the variety of personalities and professions, there are a few special friends with whom you can identify—friends who are just waiting to help you along the way.

Throughout *Girlfriends and Other Saints*, I will share how the saints—like St. Teresa of Avila and St. Catherine of Siena—were friends who literally came marching into my life just when I needed them the most. And let's not forget the queen of all saints: the Blessed Mother.

My hope is that as you read this book, you will come to see why any friend of God can and wants to be a friend to you and me.

CHAPTER 1

Knocking on Heaven's Door

THE GIFT OF SAINTLY FRIENDSHIP

It's the friends you can call at 4 a.m. that matter.
—Marlene Dietrich

I wasn't feeling very valiant—far from it, actually, especially by St. Teresa of Avila's standards. There I was at home, asking God for a sign that everything was going to be okay, and asking for the additional help of my favorite and patron saint, Teresa of Avila. When I think back on the quick and direct response to prayer that I received, it still brings tears to my eyes and causes those with whom I share the story to get the chills. So that's where we will start in *Girlfriends and Other Saints*.

What I really felt like that day was a coward, all the more so because it was Holy Week—Holy Thursday, to be exact. It was almost three o'clock in the afternoon when I felt a huge wave of panic and fear come over me. What had I just agreed to? In a few hours, I would go to Mass, and then my husband and I would head out to a local TV studio where I would take part in a live half-hour talk show discussing religious freedom and gay rights. I would be appearing on the program with a gay-rights activist and a Catholic lawyer.

If you know anything about my background as a broadcast journalist, being fearful about one short interview might sound downright silly. I have been on radio and TV, as I always say, "since dirt," or for more than three decades. So one half-hour live interview should have been no big deal, right? This wasn't my first rodeo, as the old saying goes. Well, in most cases, the answer to that question would be yes, except for the fact that this talk show would be a follow-up interview to a hostile exchange I had had with a reporter from the same station a few days before.

The news story had featured me as the token Christian supporting the Religious Freedom Restoration Act. Although I knew the reporter who did the original story, it was the most hostile interview I had ever done, and I do secular interviews regarding faith-based issues quite regularly. I will spare you all the gory details, but the story was such a major hatchet job that quite a number of viewers complained after it aired as the lead on the station's evening news that night. It was pretty obvious that the reporter was either fearful of or on the side of the activist groups, or maybe both. The complaints must have been substantial, as they resulted in several written apologies from the reporter and TV management as well as another invitation to come on the air.

Given the fact that apologies from the secular press are, to say the least, a rarity and that I was being given another chance to try and inject at least a little bit of fact into what had become, for the most part, fiction, I accepted. As the time grew closer, however, so did my level of stress and fear. I specifically remember pacing back and forth in my hallway trying to drown out all the questions that kept coming to mind. "What if this is just a setup? Maybe the reporter wants his revenge after being forced to apologize for his story. What if they use the thirty minutes to do nothing but mock the Catholic Church and don't give me and the Catholic attorney a chance to speak our minds? Maybe they are just throwing us out there as tokens to show their attempt at being fair and balanced."

I continued to pray. I told God that I was ashamed and embarrassed by my weakness. It was Holy Week, after all. Christians around the world were about to mark Jesus' excruciatingly painful passion and death, and here I was, getting myself all in a tizzy over one lousy TV appearance. I begged for forgiveness, for assistance, and then again for a sign that I would be able to make Jesus proud by defending and explaining the truth. I can remember saying out loud, "St. Teresa, please help me. You're my girl. You encountered all kinds of challenges in your efforts to spread the gospel. Tell Jesus I need to know that everything is going to be okay!"

Within seconds of crying out to the heavens, I heard the mailman on my front porch. Relieved that there was something to take my mind off my misery, I opened the door and went to the mailbox. I noticed a small package and brought it inside with the rest of the mail. The package was from a lovely listener of mine from another state. Paula had sent me a beautiful letter at Christmastime, letting me know that she was an avid listener to my radio program and that she prayed for me daily. Her letter was one of the most thoughtful notes I had ever received in my years on Catholic radio.

"How sweet," I thought to myself. "An Easter gift from Paula." I had no idea what a gift I was about to receive. When I opened the box, I burst into tears and then began to laugh out loud. The contents of the gift were such an astonishingly direct answer to my prayers. The first words I saw as I removed the wrappings were "Let nothing disturb you: Teresa of Avila." The Lord and St. Teresa knew just how much of a basket case I really was that afternoon and used my spiritual sister, Paula, to save the day and the interview.

These words were on a card that came with a lovely bronze sculpture of the saint.

> This sculpture embodies St. Teresa of Avila's statement "Let nothing disturb you." Teresa, one of the greatest Christian theologians, also wrote poetry. The lines "Let nothing disturb you, / nothing frighten you, / all things pass away, / God never changes" are from one of her best-known poems. In the context of Teresa's overall thought, the lines refer to what she saw as the underlying goodness in the universe: though we may pass through difficulties large and small, this ultimate goodness is always there, and thus, we should let nothing disturb us.

Again, I kept laughing and crying at the same time, utterly amazed at God's goodness, timing, and incredible attention to detail. The Lord knows how much I love St. Teresa. Her famous poem is all over my office in various forms in both Spanish and English. It has always given me comfort. But it was the last thing I expected to see that afternoon and, in particular, right after I had asked for help from both Jesus and Teresa, the great mystic. I was so excited that I ran to my laptop to thank Paula via a Facebook message. A little while later, she wrote back, astonished that the gift had arrived when it did, since the worker at her local post office had insisted that it would arrive—at the earliest—on Holy Saturday, some two days later. Coincidence? I think not.

The sculpture now sits in a prominent place in my home office with the card and the personal note from Paula nearby on my bulletin board. As if the words from St. Teresa's famous prayer and poem weren't encouraging enough, Paula's note was filled with one encouraging line after the next. She had no way of knowing what I was going through that day, but here again, the words were another answer to prayer and a way-over-the-top gift from God.

Dear Teresa,

Knowing how much you love St. Teresa of Avila, when I saw this saint's statue, I could not help but think of you. Please place it on your desk at the studio when you question if your calling—your answer to God's call—is making a difference. You are! Your perseverance and tenacity inspire me and countless others.

The final icing on the cake was, quite frankly, as I often like to say, just God "showing off" and revealing how much he wants to shower us with his overwhelming love and generosity. In addition to the beautiful statue, Paula had also included a bracelet with a Benedictine blessing that is well-known in the Church, as it said on the card, as "armor for the spiritual battlefield": "Praying God and his angels will daily guard you in every way."

Talk about getting just the right help at just the right time! And isn't that what true friendship is all about? We're supposed to be there for one another along this journey called life. So remember that when we knock or, in my case, pound on heaven's door, we might just be very pleasantly surprised to see that the saints will and do answer us.

Oh, and if you're wondering how the interview went, thanks to a little help from some very special friends, I made it through with flying colors, and in the end, the truth won out!

That's What Friends Are For

We have probably wondered—as well as prayed about—what it would be like, heaven forbid, or what we would do if someone in our family were suddenly taken from us. Maybe we have even tried to imagine our day-to-day existence if a particular family member, for whatever reason, had never become a part of our lives. The thought, no doubt, brings us to tears and should at the same time make us more aware of the precious gift of family.

But have we ever wondered what our lives would be like without our closest friends? Think about that for a minute. I don't know about you, but just the mere thought of life without my friends gets me all choked up and brings me to my knees, thanking God for the unique gift of friendship—including the gift of saintly friends!

If we were to look up the definition of the word "gift," we would learn that it is synonymous with the word "present," as in an item someone freely gives without payment. This hits the nail on the head when it comes to what friendship is, doesn't it? Our friends are truly gifts to us. Their friendship is freely given. There is nothing quid pro quo about true friendship. We could also say that our friends, both here on earth and in heaven, are a present, or gift, to us, and are present to us in a variety of ways.

Where would I be if I couldn't talk to my friend Lynn, who lives out of state but is only a phone call or an e-mail away? Lynn and I have known each other for more than twenty-two years, after meeting on a cruise ship where we were both celebrating wedding anniversaries. We have a mutual love for the water and, more important, for Jesus, and we have grown closer through the years. Our friendship has both seen us through some stormy seas in our lives and helped us make the most of days of smooth sailing.

Where would I be without my friend Bridget, whom I have known since high school? Although she lives close by, because of our busy work and travel schedules, we only manage to see each other a few times a year for wine and a plate of sausage and peppers at our favorite Italian restaurant. But I cherish what we now call our "pepper dates." We have both been blessed with a certain amount of professional success. But because of our ties to our very humble pasts, we keep each other grounded, and our pepper dates are always a nice pick-me-up.

I am sure that you have your own share of Lynns and Bridgets: friends that are always there for you, no matter what. Even if you can't get together as often as you would like, you know they are available to you at a moment's notice.

The *Catechism* explains that just as our friends on earth are all unique, with different personalities, qualities, and experiences, so are our friends in heaven. And these unique qualities translate into an array of spiritual tools or gifts: spiritual pepper dates, so to speak, to get us through life's ups and downs and help us on this journey to heaven.

In the communion of saints, many and varied *spiritualities* have been developed throughout the history of the churches. The personal charism of some witnesses to God's love for men has been handed on, like "the spirit" of Elijah to Elisha and John the Baptist, so that their followers may have a share in this spirit. A distinct spirituality can also arise at the point of convergence of liturgical and theological currents, bearing witness to the integration of the faith into a particular human environment and its history. The different schools of

Christian spirituality share in the living tradition of prayer and are essential guides for the faithful. In their rich diversity they are refractions of the one pure light of the Holy Spirit. (2684)

That's why I can't imagine my life without St. Teresa of Avila, whom I discovered in Catholic grade school when the nuns told me all about her. St. Teresa and I go way back, as you will read in more detail later in this book. Like my friend Bridget, I feel as if St. Teresa knows me better than most because she has been with me for the long haul, from my days as a baby Christian. For some reason, I even felt close to her when I was far away from the Church.

Other saints were introduced to me through my travels or unique experiences and have also become an integral part of my life, just like my friend Lynn. And not all of them are women. I feel a strong connection with the great doctor of the Church, St. Augustine, a connection that became stronger during a visit to the ancient Roman seaport and present-day archeological site of Ostia Antica. Late in the fourth century, Augustine moved to Ostia from Milan to await passage back to North Africa. Ostia is the place where St. Augustine's mother, St. Monica, died. While I certainly haven't and never will obtain his level of knowledge, I identify with him because he was a late bloomer, faithwise. I fell away from my faith in college and didn't reembrace it until my early thirties. Like me, Augustine, as he writes in his famous *Confessions*, ran away from God until God finally caught him. We both went everywhere looking for love in all the wrong places. As I walked through the ruins of Ostia, I could sense Augustine's great grief over the loss of his mother, who never stopped praying for her wayward son. And I could hear Augustine's beautiful words of remorse and gratitude to God for being lost and then found.

> I have learnt to love you late, Beauty at once so ancient and so new! . . . You were within me, and I was in the world outside myself. I searched for you outside myself, and disfigured as I was, I fell upon the lovely things of your creation. You were with me, but I was not with you. The beautiful things of this world kept me far from you and yet if they had not been in you, they would have had no being at all. You called me; you cried aloud to me; you broke my barrier of deafness. You shone upon me; your radiance enveloped me; you put my blindness to flight. You shed your fragrance about me; I drew breath and now I gasp for your sweet odor. I tasted you, and now I hunger and thirst for you. You touched me, and I am inflamed with love for your peace.[2]

The Gifts That Help Us

Another definition of the word "gift" refers to a special talent or natural endowment. When we get to know the saints, we tend to turn to them, asking for their intercession for specific needs in our lives. That's because during the time they walked the earth, they each possessed, as we all do, certain gifts or talents. In the cases of the saints, they happened to have an overabundance of gifts. St. Peter, you might say, had among his many gifts an overabundance of "open mouth, insert foot" and "shoot first, ask questions later" syndromes. You might be thinking, "These sound a lot more like curses than gifts." But think again!

So many Christians, myself included, identify with St. Peter because he stumbled and struggled. He truly did love Jesus, but so many times his humanity got in the way. One minute Peter was open to the Holy Spirit speaking through him. When Jesus asks the disciples, "Who do you say that I am?" Peter replies confidently, "You are the Messiah, the Son of the living God." Jesus then tells Peter he is the rock on which he will build the Church. But just a few verses later, Jesus is telling the same Peter to "Get behind me, Satan!"— this, after Peter refuses to accept the fact that Jesus has to die to save the world (Matthew 16:15, 16, 23). His fear also gets the best of him during the Lord's trial before the Sanhedrin on Holy Thursday, causing him to deny Jesus three times (26:69-75). So Peter's faults, for me personally, are special gifts. As St. Paul tells us in Romans 8:28, "All things work for good for those who love God, who are called according to his purpose."

St. Peter was and is gifted in helping us realize that our mistakes can be redeemed. If Peter, who made so many mistakes, could turn his life around to the point that he was chosen by Jesus to be the first pope, then there is hope for all of us. That's why St. Peter is a friend of mine. He is someone to whom I can truly relate. With all his stumbles and fumbles, in the end he gave himself over for the Lord and the Church. The fair-weather-friend approach that he often had with Jesus was long gone. I don't know about you, but someone with a totally self-giving approach to life and relationships sounds like a pretty good pal to keep around!

Yes, I know I certainly have a friend in Jesus. I know that so much more because of my relationship with the saints. The communion of saints is truly a gift—one of the many ways our Lord shows us that he really meant it when he promised, "I will never forsake you or abandon you" (Hebrews 13:5). He is a God who keeps his promises in so many wonderful ways!

CHAPTER 2

CAN WE TALK?

HOW THE SAINTS HELP US GET REAL WITH GOD

For prayer is nothing else than being on terms of friendship with God.

—St. Teresa of Avila

We've all had them: days when we are at the end of our rope, days when we want to do our best Popeye-the-Sailor-Man imitation, look up to heaven, and yell, "That's all I can stands, and I can't stands no more." We may want to do just that, but often we don't, for a variety of reasons.

Maybe we still see God as a mean old man who will strike us with lightning if we dare to express our frustrations. Maybe we feel that God has already done so much for us that we have no right to ever question, cry out, or, to put it more bluntly, complain. Or maybe we have just come to view prayer in a more formal, structured sense in which sitting down and entering into a conversation doesn't seem, well, all that natural or normal. Whatever we have come to think or believe regarding a life of prayer, if there is one thing that the saints can and do teach us, it's how to really talk to the Lord. Or in other words, as this chapter subtitle says, how to "get real with God."

In terms of being real with God, St. Teresa of Avila is probably at the top of the list. She was confident enough, not only in the Lord's love for her, but also in her love for him, to clearly express how she was feeling when it came to the struggles of the ministry to which God had called her. Reforming the Carmelite order was no easy task. One of the best-known stories handed down through the generations has to do with this famous statement: "Lord, if this is the way you treat your friends, no wonder you have so few." This blunt and quite sarcastic comment was blurted out by the first female doctor of the Church after she had run into some major roadblocks (literally) on one of her many cross-country trips traveling the rough byways of Spain. Some versions have her being thrown from her donkey smack down into the mud. Other stories have her traveling in a wagon that had suddenly tipped over, tossing her out into the messy and not-so-friendly terrain. You can almost see her roll her eyes, look up to heaven, and ask, "Seriously, Lord?"

And, when it comes to getting real with God, let's not forget Moses. The Old Testament Book of Exodus describes Moses, the great hero who led the Israelites out of Egypt, as a friend of God: "The LORD used to speak to Moses face to face, as a person speaks to a friend" (33:11).

At one point in those very tumultuous forty years in the desert, Moses had had about enough of the Israelites and their constant whining about how things were so much better back in Egypt, even though they were slaves there. (How quickly we forget!) Here God had given them sign after sign, including their miraculous exodus out of Egypt, not to mention the parting of the Red Sea. That was a pretty big deal, wasn't it? But they grumbled and complained, always focusing on their hardships. Talk about spoiled, ungrateful children! Instead of punishing them when they complained about the very limited menu items offered at the local desert diner, the Lord offered them just what they needed on a daily basis. This was not some measly side dish but the main course, as in bread from heaven.

> Then the LORD said to Moses: I am going to rain down bread from heaven for you. Each day the people are to go out and gather their daily portion; thus will I test them, to see whether they follow my instructions or not. On the sixth day, however, when they prepare what they bring in, let it be twice as much as they gather on the other days. (Exodus 16:4-5)

Their response was nice while it lasted, but it didn't last very long. Pretty soon the same old bread every morning—even though it arrived like clockwork and from God himself no less—became boring for the Israelites, and they began complaining all over again, talking about how much better life was under Pharaoh. Okay, so they were in total bondage, but hey, at least they had fresh veggies and plenty of meaty main courses from which to choose. How bad was it really? This is where Moses begins to sound a lot like St. Teresa, and vice versa.

> When Moses heard the people, family after family, crying at the entrance of their tents, so that the LORD became very angry, he was grieved. "Why do you treat your servant so badly?" Moses asked the LORD. "Why are you so displeased with me that you burden me with all this people? Was it I who conceived all this people? or was it I who gave them birth, that you tell me to carry them at my breast, like a nurse carrying an infant, to the land you have promised under oath to their fathers? Where can I get meat to give to all this people? For they are crying to me, 'Give us meat for our food.' I cannot carry all this people by myself, for they are too heavy for me. If this is the way you will deal with me, then please do me the favor of killing me at once, so that I need no longer face my distress." (Numbers 11:10-15)

Wow! Moses, known as a friend of God, and St. Teresa, the great mystic and doctor of the Church, really tell it like it is—or like it was for them. I don't know about you, but I find this comforting and refreshing at the same time: Moses basically telling God, "Kill me now because I just can't take it anymore," and St. Teresa saying, in essence, "Lord, you have got to be kidding me. I am going all over the place trying to do your will, and this is the thanks I get?"

Finding the Balance

We are called to emulate the saints. That said, seeing great teachers such as Moses, St. Teresa, and many others getting real with God is not a license to use our prayer time to do nothing but complain. A compelling look at how to find the right balance when it comes to getting real with God was given in a beautiful reflection in the daily devotional *The Word Among Us*. My husband and I have been using this devotional to pray the daily Mass readings together for years, so this is not just a shameless plug for the publisher of this book. The reflections in *The Word Among Us* are very helpful when it comes to applying Scripture and Church teachings to our everyday lives.

This particular reflection, from August 3, 2015, focused on the first reading for the Mass that Monday, which was from the Book of Numbers, the same reading mentioned previously.

Moses showed no pretense. He didn't put on an act. So when the people were complaining and Moses was at the end of his rope, he told God so. He understood that God knew him inside and out, so what was the point of putting on a façade? Moses knew he couldn't handle the people's problems himself. So he confidently poured out his feelings to God, as he would to any friend. And because he spoke so freely, God was able to help him.[3]

King David, the same reflection points out, is another great member of that cloud of witnesses who laid it all out there before the Lord during his time on earth. David also helps us find a balance between too much grumpiness and too little honesty:

One good way to find that "sweet spot" between honesty and whining is to consider Psalm 13. David is frustrated with God, feeling cut off from the Lord; but in the end, he finishes with a statement of faith: "How long, LORD? Will you utterly forget me? . . . But I trust in your mercy. Grant my heart joy in your salvation" (Psalm 13:1, 6). Even if you feel that your faith is weak, tell the Lord that you still believe in him. Just think how pleased he is when you lean on him, even in the midst of struggle![4]

In the New Testament, we find St. Martha, who has gotten a bad reputation over the centuries for being the one who just didn't get it when it came to having her priorities in order. In St. Luke's Gospel, we read how Jesus and his disciples are traveling and stop at the home of Martha and Mary. Mary sits at the feet of Jesus, lovingly listening to every word, while Martha is busy in the kitchen, trying to get the pita bread and falafel on the table. She is getting more steamed at her sister by the minute, and she is not all that happy with Jesus either, wondering why he just doesn't seem to care about how hard she is working to be hospitable: "Lord, don't you see that Martha has left me to do all the work by myself? Tell her to help me" (cf. Luke 10:40).

Jesus replies, "Martha, Martha, you are anxious and worried about many things. There is need of only one thing. Mary has chosen the better part and it will not be taken from her" (Luke 10:41-42).

We often leave Martha right there in the kitchen with her sister and the Lord, seeing it as an "aha" or "gotcha moment" for all the anal-retentive and obsessive-compulsive types in our lives. We tend to maximize and celebrate Mary's actions and minimize or criticize Martha's words. But have we ever stopped to ponder the fact that Martha was being very honest with the Lord? Don't we all want to admit that at times we have felt the same way as Martha did with the "Marys" in our own lives? We might not be the neatest person in the world or become the next Chopped champion on the Food Network, but maybe we feel as if we are being forced to carry the majority of the workload in other areas of our lives. Maybe it's childrearing. Perhaps there are some at the office that do the least amount of work but seem to be management's favorite. Martha needs to be taken out of the box and reexamined, especially when we see her interacting with Jesus in other, much more dire situations. Most notable here is her response to Jesus concerning the death of her brother, Lazarus.

> When Jesus arrived, he found that Lazarus had already been in the tomb for four days. Now Bethany was near Jerusalem, only about two miles away. And many of the Jews had come to Martha and Mary to comfort them about their brother. When Martha heard that Jesus was coming, she went to meet him; but Mary sat at home. Martha said to Jesus, "Lord, if you had been here, my brother would not have died. [But] even now I know that whatever you ask of God, God will give you." Jesus said to her, "Your brother will rise." Martha said to him, "I know he will rise, in the resurrection on the last day." Jesus told her, "I am the resurrection and the life; whoever believes in me, even if he dies, will live, and everyone who lives and believes in me will never die. Do you believe this?" She said to him, "Yes, Lord. I have come to

believe that you are the Messiah, the Son of God, the one who is coming into the world." (John 11:17-27)

Could it be that Martha's deep faith and trust in God, which she exhibited here before the raising of her brother, Lazarus, from the dead, was what had allowed her to be so brutally honest with Jesus as she was busy preparing dinner? Can we talk? Well, Martha certainly could, because when it came to talking to the Lord, she didn't hold back. Jesus used her honesty and comfort level in these different situations to share some deep insights into the love of God—his love for her and for all of us. He did the same with Moses, St. Teresa, and King David.

We have a long way to go in our efforts to be more like these great men and women of God. But if we can't be honest and really talk with our friends, be they canonized saints or otherwise, then what kind of friends or companions along our faith journey do we really have?

CHAPTER 3

They Can Hear You Now

ENGAGING THE COMMUNION OF SAINTS

*Therefore I ask blessed Mary ever-Virgin, all the Angels
and Saints, and you, my brothers and sisters,
to pray for me to the Lord our God.*
—The Confiteor

"Why do you pray to dead people?" That was one of the
"gotcha" questions that my friend Steve Ray would use to
try and get Catholics "saved." As Steve explains in his conversion story, he assumed Catholics were all going to hell
because they regularly took part in silly, even pagan, practices
such as trying to communicate with the dead. He thought he
was doing Catholics a big favor with that type of question—
a question that unfortunately still catches many Catholics
off guard.

Somewhere deep down in our souls, however, we know the question is wrong because it assumes the saints are truly dead. Yet many of us still don't know how to answer the question. We have a hard time grasping for a verse from the Bible to explain and confirm our strong belief in the communion of saints.

Fast-forward twenty-plus years, and you'll hear and see Steve Ray, the well-known Catholic convert, author, and motivational speaker, respond to that awkward question with another question: "Where does it say in the Bible that the saints are actually dead?" When you stop and think about it, intercessory prayer involving the saints is one of the easiest teachings of our faith to explain and defend, even using Scripture. When we say we are Christians, we are saying that we believe in life everlasting. Our bodies break down and decay; eventually, we are all going to die. But our souls live on forever. The Book of Revelation speaks of "bowls full of incense" as the "prayers of the saints" (5:8, RSV), clearly pointing out that those who have gone before us are around the heavenly throne praying for us. "Bowls full of incense" implies that these prayers are a beautiful, holy scent rising up to God.

There are countless other verses reminding us that we are pilgrims on a journey and that our permanent home is with Jesus and his followers in heaven, including these words from the Lord himself in the Gospel of St. John: "Whoever believes in the Son has eternal life" (3:36).

Jesus also spoke with "dead people"—Moses and Elijah—during his transfiguration. The Old Testament tells us that Moses died at the ripe old age of 120: "In the land of Moab, Moses, the servant of the LORD, died" (Deuteronomy 34:5). Elijah, according to 2 Kings 2:11, "went up to heaven in a whirlwind." However, all three synoptic Gospels recount a conversation between Jesus, Elijah, and Moses. St. Luke writes, "Two men were conversing with him, Moses and Elijah, who appeared in glory and spoke of his exodus that he was going to accomplish in Jerusalem" (9:30-31). So getting back to my friend Steve Ray's response, if Jesus talks to "dead people," then why can't we?

I consider myself blessed to be a cradle Catholic, one who grew up in the Church, but I have to say that much of what I have learned comes from converts to Catholicism. Mark Shea is another one of those amazing converts: an author, blogger, and speaker who, like Steve Ray, does a great job of explaining and defending the faith he used to reject and criticize. Mark says engaging the saints means having them as our unseen prayer partners.

As it is on earth, so it is in heaven. The saints in glory are like Jesus in all things (as Scripture insists). Therefore, they are like him in his desire and power to love and help their brothers and sisters, especially now that they, like Christ, sit at the right hand of the Father. As Jesus spends his love "interceding for us at the right hand of the Father," so *all* the blessed dead (who desire in all things to be like him) do too. For God has shared his communal nature of love with them and with us alike.[5]

We have been talking a lot about the communion of the saints, but there is a beautiful paragraph in the *Catechism of the Catholic Church* that focuses on communion *with* the saints, which gives us an idea of how this intercessory prayer thing is supposed to work. It's not about conjuring up spirits or trying to contact those who have passed on to see into the future, which the Church forbids. It's about asking for help. We ask our Christian friends here on earth to pray for us. We believe those prayers will somehow make a difference because our friends have faith, love Jesus, and are close to him. How much closer to God are our friends in heaven! So why not, as the *Catechism* explains, get them in on the prayer chain too?

Exactly as Christian communion among our fellow pilgrims brings us closer to Christ, so our communion with the saints joins us to Christ, from whom as from its fountain and head issues all grace, and the life of the People of God itself. (957)

A "Holy Two-by-Four"

Sometimes that communion with our fellow pilgrims in heaven is made manifest through what I like to refer to as a "holy two-by-four upside the head." Despite all that God has done and continues to do for me, I sometimes need that subtle-as-a-baseball-bat reminder that the saints are real and that they do, indeed, intercede for us.

When I first began to read the Bible, I can remember wondering how the apostles could have so many doubts about Jesus when he was right there in their midst, calming the storms, raising the dead, healing the sick, and multiplying the loaves and fishes. What more did they need, for crying out loud, to get that Jesus was God? Did they need—you guessed it—a holy two-by-four upside the head or what? In answer to that last question, yes, they apparently did—and more often than not, as I continue to learn on my journey of faith, so do I. One of the most memorable "holy smacks" came during a special event in the Church that I was privileged to attend and cover.

It was the spring of 2014, and I was cohosting a pilgrimage to Rome for the canonizations of John Paul II and John XIII. During this trip, I was really looking forward to joining hundreds of thousands of pilgrims in Rome and millions on worldwide TV as we all took time to honor two giants of the faith who were being recognized as saints. Imagine my surprise when I received a profound affirmation concerning the intercession of the saints, an affirmation that didn't come from either of the two new saints who were the center of attention that week.

The feast day of another one of my favorite saints, St. Catherine of Siena, is on April 29 and fell during the middle of our trip, two days after the canonizations. I was still in Rome completing the pilgrimage and covering all of the related activities. In addition to doing live radio shows and filing regular reports for Ave Maria Radio and EWTN, I also joined the pilgrims each day for several hours as they toured Rome.

When I woke up on April 29, I was superexcited. I knew it was St. Catherine's feast day, and I couldn't wait to make my way over to Santa Maria sopra Minerva, where she is buried. On her feast day, the church actually allows people to pray inside her tomb. However, the special visit with St. Catherine would have to wait until later in the afternoon, after my radio show and pilgrimage commitments. As the day went on, I was getting more and more anxious. I just didn't know how I would make it over to the church. The clock was ticking, and there was still so much work to do. And then there were the crowds that I knew would add to an already iffy scenario.

Normally the jaunt to Santa Maria sopra Minerva from the area around the Vatican where I was stationed is only about a fifteen- to twenty-minute cab ride, but given the enormous number of people in town, a normally packed and busy Rome was even more crowded than usual. Cabs weren't easy to come by, and if you were lucky enough to find one, you could be stuck in traffic going nowhere fast. I kept praying to St. Catherine, but no matter how many prayers I said or how hard I tried to get to her tomb, it looked like it was not going to happen.

In addition to everything else I was doing, I had also agreed to be interviewed by the secular media, an NBC-TV affiliate, for a special on Pope Francis that would air in Detroit. Having given up by then on the idea of having my special visit with St. Catherine, I packed up at the Rome bureau of EWTN and made my way over to St. Peter's Square, where the interview was scheduled to take place. Off I went with my big, fat pity party in full swing.

When I arrived at the square, the producer explained that he wanted to find another location to record the interview, as so many of their segments had already been shot in front of St. Peter's. We began moving toward the Tiber River, down the famous Via della Conciliazione, the main avenue stretching for a good mile or longer in front of the Vatican. As we were moving along making small talk, I was still feeling sorry for myself. At the same time, I was apologizing to St. Catherine for not making it to her tomb to pray and to pay my respects. I was also asking for her help with the interview. The segment of the TV special for which I was being interviewed would focus on women in the Church. I had my concerns, given what that topic often means from a secular perspective. But who better to help me answer questions on women in the Church than one of the greatest, St. Catherine?

When we finally made it to our location, I couldn't believe what I saw: a larger-than-life statue of St. Catherine right in front of me. The camera was positioned toward the river, which meant I was facing the opposite direction and looking right at the statue, which is just to the left of Castel Sant'Angelo. I have been to Rome dozens of times but had only seen this remarkable statue once before, during another one of my "St. Catherine moments." To say I had a major case of the chills would be a great understatement. Given what I was feeling and that this was her feast day, it was hard to pass this off as mere coincidence. Okay, so my experience wasn't miraculous, and it probably wouldn't have been good evidence for the cause of beatification or canonization of Catherine, but it certainly was an answer to my prayers. It was, and is, a reminder that the saints are real and that they are looking for all kinds of ways to show us how much God loves us.

Just to make sure I wasn't being overly dramatic, I sought the opinion of my husband, who is a deacon, along with a dear friend of mine, Fr. Scott Courtney from the

Diocese of Lincoln, Nebraska. Both assured me that I was not losing my mind or making too much of the experience, especially since there are a thousand places to record great video and take breathtaking pictures in the Eternal City. It just so happened that we ended up right in front of the saint upon whom I had been calling for hours, and on her feast day no less. Fr. Scott reminded me of a powerful Scripture verse that tells us how much God cares for us, even in the little things: "Look at the birds in the sky; they do not sow or reap, they gather nothing into barns, yet your heavenly Father feeds them. Are not you more important than they?" (Matthew 6:26).

Fr. Scott is the one who originally introduced me to the "holy two-by-four" concept. What I really appreciate about him is his willingness to cut to the chase with me. He is loving but direct and reminds me how stubborn I can be and how quickly I forget all that God does for me and for each and every one of us, especially through the intercession of the saints. It's probably no surprise, then, that Fr. Scott describes my "St. Catherine moment" in Rome as yet one more loving but firm "two-by-four upside the head."

When we combine Church teachings with those "holy two-by-four" moments, the understanding of saints as true companions on our journey of faith—friends who are always ready to intercede for us—really begins to click.

CHAPTER 4

EVERY SAINT HAS A PAST, EVERY SINNER HAS A FUTURE

FINDING COMMON GROUND WITH THE SAINTS

I have been all things unholy.
If God can work through me, he can work
through anyone.

—St. Francis of Assisi

It's not something that automatically comes to mind when we think about great and much-loved saints like St. Francis of Assisi. We are likely to imagine Francis as the always-peaceful and oh-so-humble man who gave up everything to serve the needy, live a life of prayer, and commune with nature in the beautiful Italian countryside. When we think of Francis, we might envision him walking through the Umbrian woods in sandals and tattered robes or feeding the birds and acting as a sort of medieval Dr. Dolittle, talking and kibitzing with the animals. No doubt we have also heard about his zeal for the Lord and his efforts to rebuild the Church, which began after he heard a specific call from the Lord. We forget that St. Francis, like many saints, had quite a colorful past, to say the least.

Francis, the Christian reformer, would have been basically unrecognizable by his friends and family because his new calling, ministering to the unwanted and underprivileged, was quite the opposite of his former days as an indulgent and rebellious youth. His father was a wealthy cloth merchant who owned land around Assisi. By the time Francis was in his early teens, his party-hardy and self-centered approach to life caused him to, among other things, drop out of school and break the city curfew one too many times.

It wasn't until he was captured during a military battle and held for ransom that he ever so slowly started to change. While in prison, he began to receive visions from God. When he was finally released, he returned to his hometown a different man. Encountering a leper, he believed the man was actually Jesus in disguise. Instead of just passing him by, as he normally would have, he embraced him. His life of luxury suddenly lost its appeal, and his experience of God's love caused him to leave his wealthy heritage behind. The rest, as they say, is history.

You might be thinking, as you struggle with moderation and balance, that there are more temptations in today's world than there were in the past. Or you might believe that a particular issue or challenge you face was never a problem for all of those holy men and women who have gone before us. Well, think again. Plenty of the saints who now have churches, cities, and countless people named after them did not start out as "saintly types." This is something to take very seriously and keep close to our hearts as we journey toward Christ. The struggles of the saints have helped me realize all the more how much we can relate to them and how much they understand the struggles we all face.

Granted, the temptations may come at us in different ways and much more frequently in our 24/7 media-saturated and oversexualized culture. For example, whenever I discuss the issue of pornography or other sexual sins on my radio show, I always hear from men and women who are looking for hope and healing. Pornography addiction, in particular, is at epidemic proportions, according to countless priests I've interviewed who say it is the number one sin brought up in confession.

But when you come right down to it, as it says in the Old Testament Book of Ecclesiastes, "there is nothing new under the sun" (cf. 1:9). The great teacher, bishop, and Church father St. Augustine of Hippo had a child out of wedlock and continued to struggle with sexual temptation for many years as he was making his way toward Christ. In his autobiography *Confessions*, he wrote, "Give me chastity and continence, but not yet."[6] That's why we need to understand that when we hit the sinful potholes on this road called life, we should get back behind the wheel of faith and drive as fast as we can toward our sister and brother saints. The saints are among the helpful signposts that enable us to navigate life's often very confusing and demanding highway. After all, there are plenty of major bumps in the road that can bring our lives to a screeching halt and take us completely off course.

The Long and Arduous Journey

Just a few years after the death of St. Francis, in a nearby part of Umbria, Italy, lived a beautiful and wealthy woman now known as Blessed Angela of Foligno. Angela is the patron of those afflicted by sexual temptation. She is said to have married at an early age and had several children. By her own admission, she loved the world and its pleasures. She reportedly had a fierce contempt towards the penitents of the day, those who lived simple lives like St. Francis. These men and women sold all their belongings and spent most of their days in prayer. When they weren't praying, they were serving the Church and the poor, again like St. Francis.

Talk about God having a sense of humor! Little did Angela know that one day she, too, would become not only one of the penitents she once despised but also a Third Order Franciscan. Gradually, after seeing the fallout from Foligno's war against Perugia, she began to recognize her own sins. According to her writings, this self-examination was the real key to her eventual conversion: "It was the knowledge of sin after which my soul was deeply afraid of damnation; in this stage I shed bitter tears."[7]

Another turning point came when she apparently had a vision of hell and called upon the intercession of St. Francis. She felt St. Francis encouraging her to go to confession. She eventually sold all of her possessions, turned away from her life of luxury and leisure, and dedicated her life to serving God and bringing others to Christ and the Church.

In a General Audience in 2010, Pope Benedict XVI told the pilgrims gathered at the Vatican that while Blessed Angela is admired greatly for the spiritual heights she attained, "perhaps they give too little consideration to her first steps, her conversion and the long journey that led from her starting point, the 'great fear of hell,' to her goal, total union with the Trinity."[8]

Okay, so maybe you're not plagued by sexual or other grave sins. Maybe you'll never have enough wealth to be consumed by it, as Blessed Angela and St. Francis once were. But last time I checked, the only sinless ones to ever walk the earth were our Lord and his mother, the Blessed Virgin Mary. In other words, we all have our issues. We all "have sinned and are deprived of the glory of God," as St. Paul reminds us (Romans 3:23).

Maybe you struggle with being jealous of those who have more than you. Perhaps you are struggling in your marriage or in other relationships. Maybe you feel you're just too tired to pray or spend quality time with your family. You might be a working mom or dad who struggles with just getting through another jam-packed day of work, school, household chores, and activities. You might be among the many battling a lack of concentration during Mass or prayer time. Your sins or vices might not be nearly as dramatic as those of Augustine, Francis, and Angela. You probably didn't go around searching for and persecuting Christians like St. Paul before his conversion on the road to Damascus. But is there a saint whose struggles you can relate to? Well, as the old saying goes, "Is the pope Catholic?"

For busy moms and working women, a very recently canonized saint who was born in the twentieth century might help you. St. Gianna Beretta Molla was a wife, mother, and pediatrician. In beautiful love letters to her husband, Pietro, she often described how there never seemed to be enough time to enjoy the gifts of family life. She lamented the fact that Pietro at one point had to travel to the United States for work.

If you're the sensitive type who has a hard time with criticism, even constructive criticism, get to know St. Thérèse of Lisieux. You might be surprised that this very popular saint, who was declared a doctor of the Church, was for a time quite the emotional basket case, often bursting into tears at even the thought of someone not appreciating or admiring her. And getting back to St. Augustine, if you're angry or hurt over your own children falling away from the faith, St. Augustine's mom, St. Monica, is your go-to gal. She prayed day and night for her son and even sought the help of the archbishop of Milan, St. Ambrose. Obviously, her prayers were answered, and her perseverance paid off. The key with all of the saints is they didn't give up.

It's often said that the Catholic Church isn't a sanctuary for saints; it's actually a hospital for sinners. So we're in good company. The saints knew they had a past, some worse than others. They also knew that their past, as it says in Romans 8:28, could be used for good. St. Teresa of Avila even went so far as to suggest that our misery can be turned into ministry: "To reach something very good, it is very useful to have gone astray, and thus acquire experience."

In other words, we can learn and grow from our mistakes, however big or small. The saints were made aware of their sins but didn't get stuck in them. Instead, they focused on their future in Christ. Whatever you've done or have failed to do, hopefully one or more of the many members of the great cloud of witnesses can help you do the same. As St. Teresa said, "Praised be the Lord who has redeemed me from myself."

CHAPTER 5

The Blessed Mother Is Watching You —and Listening Too!

MARIAN DOGMA, ITALIAN-JERSEY STYLE

Jesus entrusts us to Mary as our Mother,
and Mary receives us all as her children!
—Pope St. John Paul II[9]

I was born on the East Coast—in Jersey City, New Jersey, to be exact. Shortly before my fifth birthday, my father, a mechanical engineer, was offered a position with a Detroit-area engineering firm. Even though that was fifty-plus years ago, my mother, Rosie, has never lost her Jersey accent. As a matter of fact, at ninety years of age, it seems as if her accent is even more pronounced than when we first packed the car and headed to Michigan. I have a lot of fun teasing her as well as lovingly imitating her, even with my listening audience. I even go so far as to offer "translations" for those unfamiliar with the East Coast version of certain words or phrases. "Shut the door" in my mother's language sounds more like "Shut the dawa." "Coffee" is pronounced "cawfee," and oh, how I loved to hear her say, when my dad was still alive, "Talk to your fawtha."

My mom has a strong devotion to the Blessed Mother or Blessed "Motha," as she would say. She would always remind me and my sisters as we were growing up of the importance of asking for Mary's help. We were often told to do our best to try to be more like the Blessed "Motha" in terms of the way we carried ourselves as young women. Imagine my surprise, for example, as I was leaving the house to go on one of my first dates in high school, when my mother blurted out in her ever-not-so-subtle style, "Have a good time, and rememba, the Blessed Motha is watching you." Thanks, Ma! Try pulling any shenanigans with that remark on your mind!

That was my first introduction to the beautiful teachings of the Church on Mary, Italian-Jersey style. It was simple and direct—well, more like in your face. My mother didn't need to hit me over the head with the Bible. She was just reminding me in her own Italian-American way that we have to answer to God for the way we live our lives.

There were, and are, people watching us and wanting the best for us. It's not only our parents and family members here on earth but those in heaven, with Mary, the Blessed "Motha," leading the way.

Some might think my mom's warning was nothing more than a strong dose of Catholic guilt. Okay, I have to admit that in our full-blooded Italian Catholic family, we have advanced degrees in guilt. (Rosie has a PhD and I have a master's degree.) There were times I could have sworn that my mother was also a travel agent—for guilt trips, that is. That said, I realize that her words, however annoying they were at the time, also have a lot to do with her knowledge of how much Mary, our Queen and Mother, loves us. She is watching us and wants to help us, encourage us, and comfort us.

If you're blessed, as I am, to have your mother still with you, don't you find yourself turning to her in those tough times, or even just to have a chat on an average day and to hear her voice, no matter how old you may be? How much more often should we be running to the mother of Jesus, who is our spiritual mother! The *Catechism of the Catholic Church* tells us that the Blessed Mother is watching us, and for good reason: because she is our mother "in the order of grace":

This motherhood of Mary in the order of grace continues uninterruptedly from the consent which she loyally gave at the Annunciation and which she sustained without wavering beneath the cross, until the eternal fulfillment of all the elect. Taken up to heaven she did not lay aside this saving office but by her manifold intercession continues to bring us the gifts of eternal salvation. (969)

Mary's title as Blessed Mother is right out of the pages of Scripture. In the first chapter of St. Luke's Gospel, when a pregnant Mary arrives at the home of her pregnant elderly cousin Elizabeth, the two have a beautiful exchange about the glory of God and his many gifts. Not only do we see Elizabeth recognizing Mary as the mother of God and the "most blessed among women," but we also see Mary at some level realizing the special role given to her by the Savior, the son growing in her own womb.

When Elizabeth heard Mary's greeting, the infant leaped in her womb, and Elizabeth, filled with the holy Spirit, cried out in a loud voice and said, "Most blessed are you among women, and blessed is the fruit of your womb. And how does this happen to me, that the mother of my Lord should come to me? For at the moment the sound of your greeting reached my ears, the infant in my womb leaped for joy. Blessed are you who believed that what was spoken to you by the Lord would be fulfilled."

And Mary said: "My soul proclaims the greatness of the Lord; / my spirit rejoices in God my savior. / For he has looked upon his handmaid's lowliness; / behold, from now on will all ages call me blessed. / The Mighty One has done great things for me, / and holy is his name." (Luke 1:41-49)

As my husband and I made our way back to the Catholic Church in the early 1990s, there weren't many Catholic Bible studies available, or at least they weren't being offered in our archdiocese. We had many wonderful Protestant friends who invited us to their Bible study programs. While these studies helped us grow in our love for Jesus and Scripture, because they were nondenominational, topics such as Mary, the saints, and the sacraments were never discussed. In all fairness, none of the participants during group discussions could talk specifically about their church affiliation. The exchanges before the weekly lecture were based solely on the questions provided in the outline.

So over the years, we found ourselves embracing more of a Protestant-like view of Mary and pushing her off to the side somewhere. We were still in the Church and had no intention of leaving because we truly believed in the Eucharist. But because we were focusing all of our prayers and efforts on growing closer to Christ, we didn't see a need for Mary and the saints. We didn't know all that much about the Church's teachings about the role of Mary in our lives. Occasionally, my mother's words would come to mind when I ran across a Scripture verse about the Blessed Mother, but I would quickly put any questions aside and go on with my Bible study.

She's There When We Most Need Her

Yet, like a good and patient mom, Mary was waiting for me, and she was there when I needed her most, when my father passed away years later. Eventually, some painful but profound experiences, along with those beautifully personal words of both the Blessed Mother and St. Elizabeth in St. Luke's Gospel, were the catalysts that helped me truly welcome Mary back into my life.

A lot transpired between those early years of our reversion to the Church and my father's death. We continued to study Scripture. We discovered EWTN and Ave Maria Radio. We learned about converts such as Dr. Scott Hahn and Steve Ray. We heard the testimonies of "reverts" such as Jeff Cavins and my colleague, Al Kresta. We realized the beauty and depth of our faith and fell deeper in love with each other and Jesus by getting to know his mother—our mother—and the saints. By the time of my father's death in 2010, I had been working in Catholic radio for seven years and my husband was enrolled in the diaconate program.

My father was born on March 25, the feast of the Annunciation. Hence, my grandmother gave him the middle name of "Annuziato" in honor of the Blessed Virgin. My father died on September 15, another important Marian date, the feast of Our Lady of Sorrows. This title given to Mary was based on the passion and death of Jesus but also on the words spoken by Simeon during the presentation in the temple:

> And Simeon blessed them and said to Mary his mother, "Behold, this child is destined for the fall and rise of many in Israel, and to be a sign that will be contradicted (and you yourself a sword will pierce) so that the thoughts of many hearts may be revealed." (Luke 2:34-35)

The feast day was lost on me at first. I was too busy mourning my father, and my husband and I were caught up in the flurry of difficult but necessary details of the funeral arrangements. It wasn't until one of my friends, after learning of my father's death, gave me a beautiful painting of Our Lady of Sorrows that I began to connect the dots with the date of my father's death and the involvement of the Blessed Mother.

After the funeral was over, I decided to do some research on the feast day. What I discovered took me right back to my mom's words: "Remember, the Blessed Motha is watching you." All of a sudden, it was very clear that Mary had been closely watching my father all of his life up until he took his last breath. You see, my father, who was eighty-four years old when he died, had been diagnosed with the debilitating disease of Parkinson's some ten years earlier. That, combined with heart surgery a few years later, had left him in very bad shape. Near the very end, this once very vibrant, articulate man could hardly speak or move. He was so stiff and so very tired. Prior to his physical challenges later in life, my father had very few medical issues. He also had a low tolerance for pain and discomfort. This is where Mary's watchful ways really came into play. In doing my research as I was preparing to pray the Rosary for my dad, I read on a prayer card that those who die on this feast day are promised a peaceful death. The words took my breath away, and I began to cry. We should all be blessed to pass on to the next life as peacefully as my father, Michael Annuziato Squillace, did.

On the morning of September 15, my mom had just finished giving Dad his breakfast: Italian sausage and eggs. She then helped him to his favorite chair in the living room and went down the hall to grab a brush so that she could comb his hair. As she was making her way back toward him, she noticed that his head had dropped close to his chest. She didn't panic at first because she just thought he had simply fallen asleep, which was nothing unusual, given his condition. She quickly realized that he was gone, and it had happened in less than a minute. There was no sign of any struggle or discomfort. He just sat down and went on his way to his final resting place.

Since I was very close to my father, this experience with Mary had a profound impact on me. I was able to really appreciate the important role she can play in our lives. Through the many approved Marian apparitions, the Blessed Mother is always telling us that she loves us and is our mother. Most important, she is always reminding us to take our faith seriously: to pray the Scriptures and the Rosary, to go to confession, and to make the most of the gift of her son in the Eucharist, "the source and summit" of our faith (*Catechism*, 1324).

I also find Mary's words in the Gospel of St. John at the wedding feast of Cana to be very telling: "Do whatever he tells you" (2:5). Mary, like a good mother, knows what's best for us, so she is constantly leading us back to her son. As my mom, Rosie, says, "The Blessed Motha is watching us." She kept a close watch on my father from the beginning of his life right up to his last moments on earth, and she does the same for us, if we call on her intercession. Thanks, Ma!

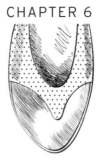

CHAPTER 6

ALL SUNSHINE MAKES
A DESERT

*The God of all grace who called you to his eternal
glory through Christ Jesus will himself restore, confirm,
strengthen, and establish you after you have
suffered a little.*

—1 Peter 5:10

"All sunshine makes a desert." It was an old Arab proverb, according to my Bible study instructor. I remember sitting in the pews of the local Baptist church more than twenty years ago and really being struck by her words as she proceeded to discuss the week's Scripture lessons, which pertained to the unpopular and painful topic of suffering. I had been back in the Catholic Church for only a short time, but I could definitely identify with the proverb's meaning. We don't really learn or grow if we don't experience some sort of discomfort. Yet when we are in the midst of the pruning, the stretching, and the dying to self, most of us—and I put myself at the top of the list—whine and complain all day long, asking God to relieve us of the very thing that he just might use to perform a miracle in our lives. We all know at some level that no one gets out of this life unscathed. It's not a matter of *if* we are going to suffer but *when*. The not-so-fun moments or periods in my life are made so much more worthwhile when I look to the Church and her saints for examples and a helping hand.

Back then, I was still trying to deal with my own set of unsettling circumstances, wondering what God was doing in my life. About a year before enrolling in that Bible study, my world had been rocked when I was unexpectedly fired from my job. I had achieved a great deal of success as a local broadcast journalist, but it almost cost me everything, because, quite frankly, everything in my life was about my career or me, myself, and I. The long hours, along with the nonstop phone calls and requests to work another weekend or holiday, had taken their toll on my marriage and my emotional and spiritual well-being. But I kept pressing on, thinking that things at home— and my stress level—would take care of themselves. Just when I thought I was reaching a high point in my career, everything was turned upside down. One night I was reporting the lead story live on the 10 p.m. news, and the next morning I was walking out of the TV station with a box of belongings in my hands. The station decided that they needed some on-air changes, and I was one of them. As I was leaving the station that day, I can remember thinking, "Now what?" My coveted career was suddenly gone, and my marriage was a mess.

Although that firing was one of the most painful things I had ever experienced, it would later turn out to be a huge blessing in disguise. When I hit rock bottom, I had nowhere to go but on my knees and back into the arms of Christ and a supportive, loving husband who, unbeknownst to me at the time, was praying for my reversion. My husband had been back in the Church for about a year, and God was preparing his heart to help me also find my way home. It was a long journey, but eventually I made it out of the dry, self-absorbed place where I had been living for years.

Indeed, all sunshine does make a desert. No guts, no glory. No cross, no crown. Rain is needed to make the flowers grow. If we're honest with ourselves, we can look back over our lives and realize that important lessons are learned most frequently from disappointments, mistakes, interrupted plans, and even tragedies, big and small. Suffering often brings us to the proverbial fork in the road where we have to make key choices.

What Should I Learn from This?

The saints have taught me to use troubles or suffering for good. Of course, I'm still tempted to ask the Lord, "Why me?" But I try to say—and I admit this is still not the first thing that comes to mind when something goes wrong—"Okay, Lord, this stinks! Now show me what I am supposed to learn from this, and how I can use this pain-in-the-you-know-what to make a difference."

When it comes to looking to the saints for guidance regarding growth through suffering, well, quite frankly, take your pick—there are just so many great examples to choose from. First and foremost, the saints always looked to the cross because the cross was the ultimate Romans 8:28 situation: "All things work for good for those who love God, who are called according to his purpose."

The crucifixion of Jesus, the greatest evil, turned out to be the salvation of the world. "For God so loved the world that he gave his only Son, so that everyone who believes in him might not perish but might have eternal life" (John 3:16).

How often do we see the John 3:16 posters at football games or concerts but fail to ever stop and think about the intense suffering that came with the ultimate sacrifice for both God the Father and God the Son?

Pope St. John Paul II has helped me in so many ways wrap my mind and heart around the connection between love, life, and suffering. I have always felt close to John Paul II. It began in my college years while earning my journalism degree. Don't get me wrong—by the end of my freshman year, the only time I was going to Mass was the night before an exam, promising God that I would be good if only he would allow me to pass my latest test or finish yet another project. Other than that, the only time you would have found me in a church was at a wedding or when I went home for the holidays and felt that, out of respect for my parents, going to Mass was the right thing to do. That said, I still proudly identified myself as a Catholic, even though I was not practicing my faith.

John Paul II first caught my attention one afternoon as I was reading the latest edition of a trade journal published by the Society of Professional Journalists. The magazine, *The Quill,* was reporting on the pope's visit to the United States in 1979. In an address to reporters at the United Nations, he thanked them for their coverage and their work and reminded them of the importance of serving the truth.

You are indeed servants of truth; you are its tireless transmitters, diffusers, defenders. You are dedicated communicators, promoting unity among all nations by sharing truth among all peoples. If your reporting does not always command the attention you would desire or if it does not always conclude with the success that you would wish, do not grow discouraged. Be faithful to the truth and to its transmission, for truth endures; truth will not go away. Truth will not pass or change. And I say to you—take it as my parting word to you—that the service of truth, the service of humanity through the medium of the truth—is something worthy of your best years, your finest talents, your most dedicated efforts. As transmitters of truth, you are instruments of understanding among people and of peace among nations.[10]

I can remember reading that statement and thinking, "Wow! The pope, 'my pope,' gets it when it comes to the media." He had me at the words "servants of truth." Little did I know way back then in my college days that I would one day be actually serving the truth, as in *the* Truth, and as a Catholic rather than a secular communicator. If you want to make God laugh, tell him your plans, right? But John Paul II had grabbed my attention. I also had the opportunity as a working journalist to cover two of his visits to the United States, including the time he visited my hometown of metropolitan Detroit in 1987 and again when he visited New York in the mid-1990s. Now in my role as a Catholic talk show host, I often lead pilgrimages to Rome, and I was able to be at St. Peter's for both John Paul II's beatification and his canonization.

What struck me about the Holy Father was his ability to love the Lord and life no matter what type of evil or suffering he witnessed, either personally or in the world around him. He was always so joyful and so determined. He is probably best known for the words "Be not afraid." He first gave this exhortation during the homily at his inauguration Mass on October 22, 1978.

> Brothers and sisters, do not be afraid to welcome Christ and accept his power. Help the Pope and all those who wish to serve Christ and with Christ's power to serve the human person and the whole of mankind. Do not be afraid. Open wide the doors for Christ. To his saving power open the boundaries of States, economic and political systems, the vast fields of culture, civilization and development. Do not be afraid. Christ knows "what is in man." He alone knows it.[11]

Despite a long list of trials he endured, John Paul II never let himself be overcome by despair. He taught us how to live with dignity and joy even as Parkinson's began to take its toll on him. Instinctively, we know that good can and does come from suffering. We all have our well-earned battle scars that have helped make us who we are today. Even with such experiences, however, instead of pulling a Gene Kelly and singing and dancing in the rain, we tend to run for shelter at the first sign of one little storm cloud or raindrop. Yet when we take a closer look at the life of Pope St. John Paul II, we see that the rain showers he endured were at times more like monsoons and hurricanes.

He knew about the importance of family because he lost his immediate family at a young age. He was able to stand up to oppressive regimes and helped effect huge political change because, as a survivor of World War II and later living in a communist Poland, he knew what the loss of true freedom, including religious freedom, meant. He had great sympathy and empathy for the sick because he experienced his own share of physical pain after he was shot and seriously injured in St. Peter's Square. Our salvation, true happiness, and real freedom, he pointed out in one of his apostolic letters, cannot be separated from suffering and, in particular, the cross of Christ.

"For God so loved the world that he gave his only Son, that whoever believes in him should not perish but have eternal life" (John 3:16). These words, spoken by Christ in his conversation with Nicodemus, introduce us into the very heart of God's salvific work. They also express the very essence of Christian soteriology, that is, of the theology of salvation. Salvation means liberation from evil, and for this reason it is closely bound up with the problem of suffering. According to the words spoken to Nicodemus, God gives his Son to "the world" to free man from evil, which bears within itself the definitive and absolute perspective on suffering. At the same time, the very word "gives" ("gave") indicates that this liberation must be achieved by the only-begotten Son through his own suffering. And in this, love is manifested, the infinite love both of that only-begotten Son and of the Father who for this reason "gives" his Son. This is love for man, love for the "world": it is salvific love.[12]

Any Christian, even those with a minimal understanding of Scripture, knows that Christ never said it would be easy. He didn't say, "Take up your picnic basket and your bottle of bubbly, and follow me to a lovely beach." Quite the opposite, as John Paul II points out. Over and over again in Scripture, there are references to suffering.

> Christ did not conceal from his listeners the need for suffering. He said very clearly: "If any man would come after me . . . let him take up his cross daily" (Luke 9:23), and before his disciples he placed demands of a moral nature that can only be fulfilled on condition that they should "deny themselves" (cf. 9:23). The way that leads to the Kingdom of heaven is "hard and narrow," and Christ contrasts it to the "wide and easy" way that "leads to destruction" (cf. Matthew 7:13-14). On various occasions Christ also said that his disciples and confessors would meet with much persecution, something which—as we know—happened not only in the first centuries

of the Church's life under the Roman Empire, but also came true in various historical periods and in other parts of the world, and still does even in our own time.[13]

If Jesus, who is God and without sin, suffered intense pain, humiliation, and persecution, why do we think our lives as Christians are going to be a walk in the park or that day at the beach with the sparkling wine?

Thanks to saints such as Pope St. John Paul II, I've tried to learn at least something from my trials, most of which, by the way, have been brought on by my own stupid mistakes. But whether it's my own fault or just the way the cookie crumbles in this fallen world of ours, I've learned to try and turn obstacles into opportunities. Now when I look back at my painful experience of being let go from a prominent TV position, and when I think about all the struggles my husband and I went through in healing our marriage, I realize that without those difficulties, we would never be where we are right now: in a much better place in our relationship with each other and with Jesus.

God will restore us, as St. Peter said (cf. 1 Peter 5:10), and pain, as St. Teresa of Avila said in her famous prayer, is never permanent.

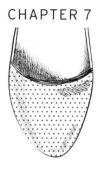

CHAPTER 7

ANYWHERE BUT THERE

A LESSON IN TOTAL ABANDONMENT

"My Father, if it is not possible that this cup pass without my drinking it, your will be done!"
—Matthew 26:42

It has always been a dream of mine to visit Avila, Spain, the home of St. Teresa. Most of the pilgrimages I lead or cohost are to Italy and the Holy Land, so when my friend Steve Ray asked me to join him on a trip to Spain, you don't have to guess how I responded!

Not only would we have the opportunity to visit the land of St. Teresa, but we were actually going to be there during the year-long, five-hundredth celebration of her birth. The celebration began on her feast day, October 15, 2014, and ended on the same date in October 2015. I couldn't wait, and I also couldn't stop thanking God for granting me such a privilege.

I tried to prepare myself as I do for other spiritual retreats. Prayer before and during the trips is obviously a must. Plus, I try to do some extra reading about the holy sights on the itinerary as well as learn more about the saints we will meet along the way. This was a great chance for me to revisit some of Teresa's many writings. I also prayed and asked St. Teresa to help me get closer to Christ. Be careful what you pray for! St. Teresa, a powerhouse of prayer and mysticism, does not let people off lightly if they are sincerely looking to love God with all of their heart, mind, soul, and strength.

All over Avila and the other towns significant in the lives of both St. Teresa and her close friend and spiritual advisor, St. John of the Cross, were lovely signs and posters with her image as well as lines from her prayers and poems. The actual theme of the celebration was built around a prayer I was not all that familiar with entitled "I Am Yours," also referred to as "In the Hands of God."

I am Yours and born for You.
What do you want of me?
Majestic Sovereign,
Unending wisdom,
Kindness pleasing to my soul:

God sublime, one Being Good,
Behold this one so vile,
Singing of her love to you:
What do you want of me?[14]

The long poem is really a love letter in which St. Teresa continually pours out her soul, telling God that she will do whatever he asks of her, no matter the cost. Our pilgrimage spiritual director, Fr. Alfonso Aguilar, a theologian, author, and now a parish priest serving in Madrid, frequently referred to the poem during his talks on the pilgrimage and also during his wonderful homilies. He reminded us that although Teresa ran into one challenge after another, not only in her efforts to reform the Carmelites, but with her health as well, once she fell in love with God, that was it— her love and devotion for him were so strong that nothing else mattered but doing his will. All during the pilgrimage, I felt St. Teresa trying to tell me that I had barely scratched the surface in my relationship with Jesus.

Avila is a stunningly beautiful walled city that sits on a hillside in the rugged but lovely Spanish countryside. I was struck not only by its stark beauty but also by its peacefulness. There are all sorts of statues and images of St. Teresa throughout the city, and there is no mistaking the strong spiritual presence of this great doctor of the Church.

Everywhere I turned, whether it was at the convent of St. Joseph, St. Teresa's first foundation, or the Monastery of the Incarnation where she spent so many years of her life and where we walked through the rooms where she lived, prayed, and ate with her Carmelite sisters, I felt her telling me to "Put out into the deep." I also found myself talking to her and saying, "What do you mean, 'put out into the deep'? Haven't I already done just that? My entire life has changed. Aren't I doing God's will?"

Of course, I was asking these questions of this spiritual giant as I was staring at her personal items displayed behind glass, including a heavy and very rough log that she used as her pillow. I had this back-and-forth conversation in my head as I listened to a local guide describe how Teresa was also known as the "walking saint" because she would often take off on foot across Spain in order to search for another property that might serve as the next convent of her reformed order. I tried to put those questions and her voice out of my mind. Quite frankly, I just didn't want to go there. I was feeling pretty darn weak to begin with. All the times I had moaned about not getting the exit row on the plane came to mind, not to mention my very comfortable American lifestyle in general. I didn't even know what or where going "there" was. It was fairly likely, for obvious reasons, that I wasn't being called to a life like hers in the convent. But there was probably a pretty good chance, based on my previous experience, that it would have to do with some sort of sacrifice or suffering. It sounded like I was going to have to move out of my current comfort zone at some level.

As I said, I am getting a little better at this suffering thing. I do ask God to show me the silver linings when the clouds roll in, the lessons he wants me to learn and apply. But I am human and still struggle. At the time of our Avila journey in the spring of 2015, I had a lot on my plate. There was a long list of different writing and TV projects, as well as my increasing responsibilities with Mom, who was beginning to need more attention due to some health issues. So again, I was just sort of hoping the Lord and his great servant, St. Teresa, would give me a break so that I could pass on whatever cup might be coming my way. Deep down I knew better. All sunshine makes a desert, right?

"What Do You Want of Me?"

I arrived home from my trip, and despite the little spiritual tug-of-war I was having with God and St. Teresa, I felt closer to both of them. One step I knew I definitely needed to take was to track down St. Teresa's "I Am Yours" prayer. So after a little research online, I found it and printed a copy for myself to read and pray with. Holy cannoli! I don't know what I was expecting, but the poem is over-whelmingly challenging. "Daunting" is a better word for it. The first few paragraphs are full of statements of love, commitment, and questions about following God's will. Okay, I can go with that. But this was over the top!

Give me death, give me life,
Health or sickness,
Honor or shame,
War or swelling peace,
Weakness or full strength,
Yes, to these I say,
What do You want of me?

And that's just for starters.

Give me wealth or want,
Delight or distress,
Happiness or gloominess,
Heaven or hell,
Sweet life, sun unveiled,
To you I give all.
What do You want of me?

Give me, if You will, prayer;
Or let me know dryness,

An abundance of devotion,
Or if not, then barrenness.
In you alone, Sovereign Majesty,
I find my peace.
What do You want of me?

Give me then wisdom.
Or for love, ignorance,
Years of abundance,
Or hunger and famine.
Darkness or sunlight,
Move me here or there:
What do You want of me?

If You want me to rest,
I desire it for love;
If to labor,
I will die working:
Sweet Love say
Where, how and when.
What do You want of me?

Calvary or Tabor give me,
Desert or fruitful land;
As Job in suffering
Or John at your breast;

Barren or fruited vine,
Whatever by your will:
What do You want of me?

Be I Joseph chained
Or as Egypt's governor,
David pained
Or exalted high,
Jonas drowned,
Or Jonas freed:
What do You want of me?[15]

It was too much for me. As I was reading it, I heard St. Teresa's voice again, telling me that I needed to be able to read her words and say yes again and again to God—to go deeper with him. This commitment to love and serve God fully is not a one time thing, even—and maybe especially—for those of us in ministry. We have to be able to face our fears and our troubles and take whatever punches come our way. We get knocked down. We get back up again. But no matter what, we keep putting ourselves in the ring for the Lord.

A Silent Retreat with St. Teresa

Instead of taking time to actually contemplate what St. Teresa and the Lord were obviously trying to tell me, I put the poem back on the shelf and went right back to my busy speaking, writing, and radio show schedule.

Two days after my pilgrimage, I was a keynote speaker at a women's conference in Connecticut. I felt a little cold coming on but ignored it and went right on with my grueling schedule. From Connecticut it was back home to do the radio show and then back out the door to another speaking engagement, this time in Kansas City for a women's conference. In the days before the Kansas City event, I could feel my voice going. I wasn't at all worried. That happens from time to time for those whose voice is their main livelihood. When I got on the plane heading for Kansas City, my voice was fine—or so I thought. Apparently, the bug was still in my system. I gave an hour-long keynote presentation, and at the end of the talk, my voice was long gone.

Of course, being the Type A personality that I am, I kept on trying to use my voice, making a bad situation even worse. I talked to the women who were purchasing my books. I talked to the nice Catholic man sitting next to me on the plane for two hours, straining to be heard over the engines. After all, he had questions about the Church and my ministry, so I just had to talk. By the time I got home, I was in very bad shape. The radio network insisted I take a break from the show for a few days to let my throat heal. But even after a few days of voice rest, there was absolutely no improvement. Now I was really worried.

I was able to get in to see my ENT doctor, a specialist who works with performers and broadcasters. The news was not good. I had severely strained my vocal chords and had a tear in one of them. He put me on complete voice rest for several weeks, which meant no talking at all: no radio show, no phone calls, and no talking, period. To make matters even more frightening, he wasn't giving me any guarantees that my voice would return to its previous strength and could not promise that life as I knew it, including broadcasting and speaking regularly, would return to normal. There might be a "new normal," whatever that meant. After several weeks of voice rest, he would take another look at my vocal chords. He also prescribed therapy with a voice pathologist to learn better breathing and voice techniques. As he explained, I was pushing myself way too hard and needed to slow down. It was something he often saw in many of his patients, especially women.

That's something that really made me stop and think. At that point, I had been in Catholic ministry for more than fifteen years. Through the grace of God, my marriage had been healed and the Lord had given me many opportunities to share my communications gifts through evangelization. However, old habits die hard. I was always very driven, to a fault. The communications industry, and broadcast news in particular, is an extremely competitive and demanding field. You don't make it without working, not just hard, but extremely hard. I had carried that same "damn the torpedoes, full speed ahead" approach to my Catholic media ministry. I had a hard time saying no and continued in some ways to live like the Energizer Bunny on steroids. I couldn't shake what had been pounded into my head by college professors, news directors, and the radical feminist movement: that it has to be all or nothing when it comes to reaching your professional goals.

Think I'm exaggerating? Well, in addition to my talks in Kansas City and Connecticut, I was also scheduled to speak in four other cities in less than a month. Then, of course, there was the daily radio show, a taping for my EWTN TV program (which included cohosting a pilgrimage in Birmingham, Alabama), and then another pilgrimage to Italy. And this didn't include personal commitments and responsibilities on the home front.

So there I was, with no voice and doctor's orders to be completely silent—definitely a new thing for me. The station was very understanding. They ran reruns of my talk show as long as they could and then brought in several of my colleagues to guest host the show when possible.

My husband and I began to communicate through texting and handwritten notes. He jokes now that those days of silence were "the good ole days."

At first, I was angry and frustrated. My voice rest began during the week the Supreme Court was hearing the case on same-sex marriage. At that same time, the riots in Baltimore broke out. It drove me crazy not to be able to cover such major stories and not to be able to comment, other than writing blogs or posting on Facebook. I was not a happy camper, but then I remembered St. Teresa's voice urging me to go deeper and thought, "Maybe I should use this as a forced silent retreat. Maybe God wants me to slow down, take a rest, and draw closer to him." Duh, d'ya think? What a concept!

And so for the next several weeks, that's what I did. Every morning, in addition to praying the daily Mass readings, I also read from my friend Dan Burke's book *30 Days with Teresa of Avila,* which is based on a collection of St. Teresa's personal letters. I also dove into *Divine Intimacy: Meditations on the Spiritual Life* by Fr. Gabriel of St. Mary Magdalen. This book is considered a Christian classic, filled with Carmelite spirituality along with meditations and reflections connected to the liturgical calendar. With the exception of playing Christian music in the background, my home was also filled with silence for the most part. Maybe it was my imagination, but every reading, every song, and every page in these two books spoke to me about trust and putting God at the center of everything. I felt a great deal of peace, but every once in a while I would start to panic and wonder what was going to happen to me if my voice failed to return fully. What would I do? What would the rest of my life be like?

That's when I decided to reread the rest of St. Teresa's prayer. The last few lines hit me like a ton of bricks.

Silent or speaking,
Fruitbearing or barren,
My wounds shown by the Law,
Rejoicing in the tender Gospel;
Sorrowing or exulting,
You alone live in me:
What do You want of Me?

Yours I am, for You I was born:
What do You want of me?[16]

"'Silent or speaking'? Maybe God really is trying to tell me something," I thought. I reached for my cell phone and texted my husband, who was just in the other room. "What if I really don't get my voice back? What's going to happen to me and the ministry God has given me?" My husband reminded me of all the fruit I was gaining through this forced silent retreat. He also reminded me how my life had been the ultimate example of how, when God closes a door, he opens not just a little tiny window, but a huge wall-to-wall window. He was referring to how God moved me from local secular media to international Catholic radio and TV, a platform I never knew existed. And then it hit me. What the heck was I worried about? God had never let me down. He had given me a new life and a renewed marriage and countless opportunities to tell others about him in the most wonderful places. Only a few weeks had passed since my Holy Week miracle, and here I was, little miss cry baby, getting all doubtful and wimpy again. Oh, ye of little faith!

I grabbed my copy of "I am Yours," took a deep breath, and read the entire prayer from start to finish. It gave me a greater appreciation of St. Teresa's no-holds-barred commitment to Christ, and it reassured me as I looked back on my life and realized that God had continued to move me from one place to the next as long as I kept saying yes to him. Whatever happened would all be in God's will. I knew that God doesn't waste the talents and treasures he gives people and that he would use me—maybe differently—but he would still use me.

My vocal chords eventually healed, and my voice came back. I was able to resume my role as a talk show host and motivational speaker. Some of my friends say that

God forced me into a silent retreat to gain strength for the many cultural battles that Christians are facing on the front lines. That could be. But I know it was also a time of self-reflection and personal growth. I had to get some balance back into my life again. I had to take better care of my voice and not say yes to every speaking engagement that came along. I had to restrict my hours on air to only the talk show and no extra assignments. These were some tough lessons that had to be learned, but I am grateful they came along.

Finally, I had to learn what St. Teresa of Avila learned and lived so well: that we need to be willing to go anywhere with God and to remember that if God takes us to it, he will see us through it.

CHAPTER 8

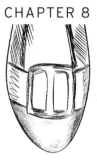

Thoughts Interrupted

UNEXPECTED BUT WELCOME VISITS FROM THE SAINTS

If anyone comes to me, I want to lead them to Him.
—Edith Stein (St. Teresa Benedicta of the Cross)

One of the important truths I have learned about prayer in my years back in the Church has been that prayer comes in all shapes and sizes. Putting our prayer life into practice looks different for each of us. Some of us may enjoy more formula-based prayer, such as reciting the Rosary or the Divine Mercy Chaplet. Others enjoy praying through the daily Mass readings or the Liturgy of the Hours. Some have a more free-form type of prayer or dialogue with God. We all have to find what works best for us.

It's amazing to realize, however, that our wonderful, generous, and merciful God hears us and responds to us even when we may not be involved in what we would consider a formal act of prayer. I had this type of experience in Rome a few years ago. It was the first time I was made aware of that enormous and wonderful statue of St. Catherine of Siena along the Tiber in the gardens of Castel Sant'Angelo.

My husband and I were walking near the Vatican. We had just wrapped up another pilgrimage and were going to spend the final night of our trip grabbing a glass of wine in the Piazza Navona and then enjoy a late dinner, or "cena," as they say in Italy. Often when I travel to Rome, I experience such a mixture of emotions. I feel so blessed to be Catholic with all of the Church's history, teaching, and, of course, the saints. But at the same time, I often get frustrated. Catholic author, Bible scholar, and convert Dr. Scott Hahn often says that "Catholics are sitting on Fort Knox, and they don't know it." Quite frequently we come across folks, even on an organized pilgrimage, who are like we once were. They don't realize the gift they have in the Church, and they take their faith for granted. Or we hear from many who are disappointed in their pastors and local bishops, past and present, who haven't done enough, in their opinion, to teach the faith.

These thoughts, as well as thoughts of St. Catherine of Siena, were running through my mind as we were walking that night. I remember standing on the corner at the end of the Via della Conciliazione and thinking to myself, "How did she do it?" How did a young illiterate girl in medieval Italy turn the world upside down? How did she become a great teacher of the faith and a spiritual consultant to Church leaders, all the way up to the pope? And how in the world did she keep her faith and her sanity when there was so much scandal among the Church leadership and the laity in the fourteenth century?

While these thoughts and questions were coming to mind, we began to cross the street. Suddenly I looked up and practically ran right into St. Catherine. I stopped in my tracks, which took my husband by surprise. "I can't believe this," I said, holding back tears. "At the exact moment I was thinking about St. Catherine, I literally run right into her. Where in the world did this statue come from, and how have we never seen it before?"

At the time I didn't consider the questioning in my head to be prayer. It was more like contemplation or reflection with a little bit of annoyance and cynicism thrown in. God, however, in his wisdom was aware of my questions, and this experience was just what I needed to get back on track. Next to this grand statue are four large bas-reliefs depicting scenes from St. Catherine's life. The large marble figure gives you the feeling that St. Catherine is urgently on the move in search of one more soul in need of Christ. The soul in need that night happened to be yours truly, and the statue of St. Catherine was just what the doctor— of the Church—ordered.

Scripture is filled with reminders that God knows what's on our heart, and lovingly and sometimes very directly addresses our ponderings. The psalms, for example, are filled with these types of verses; Psalm 34 in particular is a great example:

> I sought the LORD, and he answered me,
>> delivered me from all my fears.
> Look to him and be radiant,
>> and your faces may not blush for shame.
> This poor one cried out and the LORD heard,
>> and from all his distress he saved him. (34:5-7)

"I Was Just Thinking of You"

St. Teresa Benedicta, formerly Edith Stein, reached out to me in a similar way a few years earlier. It was the summer of 2010, and I was doing some prep work for my talk show. Part of my research was for a new book about the great convert. *Edith Stein and Companions: On the Way to Auschwitz*, by Fr. Paul Hamans, tells the chilling story of how St. Teresa Benedicta, along with hundreds of others, was arrested in Holland by Nazis and soon killed at either Auschwitz or another concentration camp.

I was well aware of St. Teresa Benedicta and her connection to St. Teresa of Avila. Stein was born into a strict Jewish home but lost her faith by the time she was in her teens and considered herself an atheist. After reading St. Teresa of Avila's autobiography, she said, "This is truth" and converted to Catholicism. In October of 2006, Pope Benedict XVI blessed a special statue of St. Teresa Benedicta at St. Peter's. "The marble figure stands next to that of St. Teresa of Jesus and shows the saint holding a cross and a Torah roll. Rabbis were also present at the blessing of the statue," Fr. Hamans writes.[17]

I have great admiration for both Teresas because they were both strong women and feminists in their own right long before modern feminist ideology was even developed. They both understand true feminism, or the "feminine genius" or "new feminism" that Pope St. John Paul II described, first in his encyclical *Evangelium Vitae* (The Gospel of Life) and later in other writings.

In transforming culture so that it supports life, women occupy a place, in thought and action, which is unique and decisive. It depends on them to promote a "new feminism" which rejects the temptation of imitating models of "male domination," in order to acknowledge and affirm the true genius of women in every aspect of the life of society and overcome all discrimination, violence and exploitation.[18]

Although St. Teresa Benedicta and St. Teresa of Avila lived and died long before John Paul II began speaking of this "new feminism," they were already witnessing to the feminine genius through their commitment to Christ, the truth, and the Church. Edith Stein was well educated. She was a writer and a philosopher who had a major influence on the women of her era, and she continues to have an impact today. She wrote extensively on the roles of women in society and, later, of women in Scripture and the Church. Once she found God, she had a clear understanding of who she was and, like St. Teresa of Avila, who Jesus was, particularly in the Eucharist. Their deep understanding and appreciation of the Real Presence of Jesus resonated with me because the Eucharist was the main reason my husband and I stayed in the Church. Oh, there are so many other beautiful elements of our faith that we loved, but in the end, if Jesus is who he says he is in the Eucharist, how could we leave?

My idea of feminism was formulated by the women's liberation movement of the seventies and eighties. This brand of feminism saw equality as something that requires women to be exactly like men, as opposed to women developing and applying their own unique gifts and talents. The two Teresas, along with John Paul II, enabled me to have a better appreciation of what it means to be truly female. I didn't have to act like men behaving badly in order to get ahead and make a difference in the world. This was a real paradigm shift for me.

Thinking of these incredible and extremely brilliant women, their witness, and everything they represented, which was so beautifully laid out in Fr. Hamans' book, really affected me. I don't know what I was expecting from the book and the interview, but I do know that several hours after the interview was over, I was still pondering the life and the witness of both saints, in particular St. Teresa Benedicta, who died a martyr for her faith at only fifty years of age.

St. Teresa Benedicta was still on my mind the next morning. I was praying the daily Mass readings, this time from the *Magnificat* devotional, only to find that the reflection for that very day was from none other than St. Teresa Benedicta of the Cross herself. The word "coincidence" might come to mind for some people, but I would beg to differ. After all, what are the chances? There are ten thousand saints in the Catholic Church! I'll admit I did at first think that there must have been a practical explanation. "Maybe it is her feast day today," I thought. "Yes, that's it. It must be." But after quickly reading the brief summary of the saint that goes along with the reflection each day, I learned that her feast day was actually August 9, the date of her death, and this was July 29. If that isn't enough to make you believe in the communion of saints, the reflection focused on how women can only truly find themselves by losing themselves in Christ and, in particular, the Eucharist.

> Whoever seeks to consult with the Eucharistic God in all her concerns, whoever lets herself be purified by the sanctifying power coming from the sacrifice at the altar, offering herself to the Lord in this sacrifice, whoever receives the Lord in her soul's innermost depth in Holy Communion cannot but be drawn ever more deeply and powerfully into the flow of divine life, incorporated into the mystical body of Christ, her heart converted to the likeness of the divine heart.[19]

These unexpected but welcome visits remind me of something beautiful that often happens with close friends or loved ones. Certainly there are times when you were thinking about, say, your brother, sister, or best friend. It might be that you hadn't spoken to them in a while. Maybe you just missed them and were reminiscing about some good times you shared when, all of a sudden, you receive a text message, or maybe a note or card arrives in the mail from the very person who was on your mind. Or the phone rings, and you say, "I can't believe I'm talking to you. I was just thinking about you this very minute."

Whether they walked among us sixty or five hundred years ago, the saints are our companions along our journey of faith. Just like a dear friend, even in our busy, noisy world, we're still connected. They reach out and touch us. They remind us that they are very much aware of the needs of God's people, and most important, our need to stay close to God himself.

CHAPTER 9

Walk a Mile in Their Sandals

GETTING TO KNOW THE STORIES
OF THE SAINTS

*God will not look you over for medals, degrees, or
diplomas, but for scars.*
—Elbert Hubbard

A few years ago on a pilgrimage to the Holy Land, I came to
a better understanding of the struggles of the early Christians.
On this particular trip, I was joined by a friend who is also
in full-time ministry, Janet Morana of Priests for Life. Since
it was Janet's first time to Israel, we decided to go a few days
earlier than the eighty-one pilgrims who would join us so that
we could be refreshed and ready to share when they arrived.

I chose the city of Jaffa, a quiet port on the Mediter-
ranean just south of Tel Aviv, for our respite. Jaffa is one

of the oldest port cities in the world and has great biblical significance. It is considered to be the port from which Jonah set sail for his encounter with the whale (cf. Jonah 1:3). Mentioned in Acts 9:36, it is the city where St. Peter raised Tabitha from the dead. Jaffa or Joppa, as it is referred to in Scripture, was also where Peter had the vision that enabled him to understand the Lord's desire for Gentiles to be included in the kingdom of God (Acts 10:1-33).

It's a jewel of a town, perched perfectly on top of a hill overlooking the sea. Today its cobblestone streets are lined with shops and art galleries. On our first night in Israel, we decided to grab a quick bite at one of the little cafés that provide an incredible view of the sea and the coastline. As we sat there enjoying our wine and hummus and trying to deal with the jet lag, I began to think about what it must have actually been like for St. Peter and the other apostles during the time of the early Church.

Travel, especially overseas travel, can be grueling, even with all our modern conveniences. A ten-hour flight is no picnic, and we were exhausted. But I couldn't stop thinking about what a day in the life of St. Peter might have looked like, since we were actually sitting right there looking at one of the places where he slept, ate, witnessed, and performed a miracle. How many of us actually consider the incredible effort preaching and traveling on foot took physically for the apostles? And then there were the spiritual challenges, trying to preach to a world that had just crucified Jesus. St. Peter and the apostles weren't exactly the most popular guys on the block and were often on the run, seeking shelter and safety from one town to the next. All of the apostles except St. John were actually martyred. St. Peter would later suffer his martyrdom, along with St. Paul, in Rome. St. Peter was crucified upside down; St. Paul was beheaded. And we think we have it tough!

Despite the obvious jet lag that comes with traveling to far-off places where the saints lived and made their mark, I would hop on a plane pretty much on a moment's notice in order to go back to the Holy Land, Rome, or any pilgrimage site in order to get to know our saints in a more up close and personal manner. It's a way we can really understand their lives and appreciate all they have done for the Lord.

How the Saints Lived

Many of the places connected to our saints are now official pilgrimage sites, and the rows upon rows of stores and other commercial ventures vie for our attention. However, beautiful basilicas and churches can also be found in these locations, along with actual structures where the saints lived or at least spent some time. One of these sites is Lourdes, France.

Growing up, I was always intrigued by the film *The Song of Bernadette,* starring Jennifer Jones in the lead role and based on the life of St. Bernadette Soubirous of Lourdes, France. Each time I watch the film, which beautifully illustrates the story of how the Blessed Mother appeared to the sickly and frail but faithful Catholic girl, I wonder how Bernadette and her family survived. It wouldn't surprise me if the phrase "dirt-poor" came about because of them. They literally were dirt-poor, and Bernadette's parents constantly struggled to feed and clothe their children.

Just beyond the hustle and bustle of Lourdes, in the foothills of the breathtaking Pyrenees mountains, pilgrims may visit two of the places where Bernadette's parents, Louise and Francois Soubirous, raised their family. One of these homes, where Bernadette was born and where she lived for ten years, was originally a water mill. Bernadette called it the "happiness water mill," but the few extremely austere rooms would make most of us wonder what the family had to be so happy about. Bernadette's description of her life in this simple dwelling is a reminder that, even at a young age, her joy came from deep within.

For her parents, however, this happiness was short-lived, as the Soubirous family would be forced to move again and again. When most of us think of families moving, we think of them going to another town, say, for a better opportunity or for the house of their dreams. Well, in the case of the Soubirous family, the moves were never about moving up or even laterally. It was all about simply surviving and having a roof over their heads. Survival at one point meant that Bernadette, her parents, and her three siblings were forced to make their home in just one room of an old damp dungeon called Le Cachot.

It was not long after the move to Le Cachot that the Blessed Mother began appearing to Bernadette near the cave at Massabielle, where the beautiful Lourdes grotto is now located. I have been to Lourdes twice, and both times as I walked along the cobblestone streets and stopped at Le Cachot and the water mill, I can remember thinking that this is the way God works: through the simplicity of a family confined to one room of a dungeon and the innocence of a little Catholic girl who was routinely sent to a trash dump to collect driftwood and fallen branches.

How many of us, even if we run into financial struggles, will ever face such severe poverty? How many of us, myself being at the top of the list, need to learn again and again that God works through the least of us, through those who aren't bogged down by all kinds of material baggage? How often during my own travels, whether for a pilgrimage or for a speaking engagement, do I get grumpy and complain about the uncomfortable plane rides, the long security lines, the weak Internet and cell-phone connections, and my long list of other annoyances? All throughout Church history, the saints were made saints through trials, tribulations, pain, suffering, and rejection. Hey, where do we sign up? But sign up they did, one after the other, as they marched through the centuries, enduring a lot more than a hostile culture and a bad hotel room in order to help fulfill the Church's mission of evangelization.

Reading about the Saints

Sometimes we might be blessed to literally follow in the footsteps of the saints by visiting the places where they lived, ministered, and died. The Holy Land, Rome, and Lourdes are just a few of the most well-known areas where we can really step back in time and experience what life might have been like for these trailblazers. But we don't even have to step outside our front door in order to get closer to the saints.

Several years ago, my spiritual director told me about the practice of *lectio divina,* which is Latin for "divine reading." Praying this way involves picking a particular section of Scripture, say a chapter or even just a few verses, and slowly reading over the words, becoming aware of all the details and putting yourself in the scene that's unfolding on the pages before you. The more time I take to read and reflect, the more it seems as if I have been transported back two thousand years ago to the time of Christ. The practice of lectio divina is designed to allow God to really speak to our hearts. God can show us what the readings mean and how they apply to our own lives. A period of prayer and reflection follow this "sacred reading." One of the benefits of this practice for me as I imagined the lives of the early Christians has been the realization that often purification comes through suffering.

I can also place myself in the time period of particular saints by reading good biographies. I especially love the biographies or hagiographies by Louis de Wohl, a gifted storyteller and devout Catholic who spares no detail in describing the lifestyles and surroundings of great saints, including Augustine, Aquinas, and Catherine of Siena. His books give us a clearer picture of the environment in which the faith journeys of the saints began and prospered.

It doesn't matter whether you let your fingers do the walking through the pages of a great book—including the best-selling book of all time, the Bible—or actually head to Israel, Italy, France, Spain, or even a place nearby that is connected to a saint. Whether you use a book, a car, or a plane ticket, walking a mile in the footsteps of our saints will definitely help you get to know them and jump-start your faith journey.

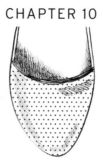

CHAPTER 10

THANK YOU FOR BEING A FRIEND

HOW FRIENDSHIP IS GOD'S WAY OF TAKING CARE OF US

*Therefore, encourage one another and build
one another up, as indeed you do.*
—1 Thessalonians 5:11

*Thank you for being a friend,
traveled down the road and back again.
Your heart is true, you're a pal and a confidant.*

*I'm not ashamed to say,
I hope it always will stay this way.
My hat is off, won't you stand up and take a bow.*

Andrew Gold's hit single "Thank You for Being a Friend" was originally released almost forty years ago, all the way back in 1978, but most remember it fondly from NBC's hit sitcom *The Golden Girls*. Singer Cynthia Lee rerecorded the tune for the show's theme song, and it stuck—both the song and the sitcom, that is. *The Golden Girls* is still in reruns all over cable TV. Even those among us who might not have been around when the program was running in its heyday from 1985 to 1992 have become familiar with the very funny and very real experiences of the smart and tough Dorothy, her feisty Sicilian mother, Sophia, the egocentric Blanche, and the flighty but adorable Rose.

I think they were and are still so very welcome in our homes via television because the characters are sincere and easy to relate to, and their relationship as friends is something that deep down we all desire and hope for. Oh sure, Dorothy at times got fed up with Blanche's obsession with her appearance. Blanche, Dorothy, and Sophia would often look at the spacey Rose with blank stares, wondering how she made it through the day, given her, you might say, "airheadedness." However, no matter what crazy circumstance they faced, no matter how many squabbles they had, the theme or plot of the show focused on their commitment to their friendship. They really seemed to care about each other.

Good friends are another one of God's great gifts to all of us. As you've read in previous pages, I am blessed by the heavenly friends I am making through the communion of saints, but I have also been blessed to have a few "golden girl"-type relationships with friends here on earth. They're golden not because of their age but because they are priceless, and as the song says, have "traveled down the road and back again" with me in good times and in bad. And while a lot of us might not be retired and living in a cute Florida ranch house with a lovely lanai where we lounge around drinking our wine or martinis like Dorothy, Sophia, Blanche, and Rose, we have our own special ways of bonding and remaining close.

Sometimes it can take us a while to appreciate or realize who our tried-and-true friends really are. If you were to look at my life when I was at the height of my news career, you would think I was the most popular girl around. My social calendar was certainly full. And there wasn't a press party, social event, or celebrity meet-and-greet that didn't have my name on the invite list. In between those glitzy and local star-studded gatherings were regular hangouts with the news crews at least once a week. Again, I considered these media types my friends. A newsroom, after all, is no place for wimps. And having others who had survived the day-to-day stress of this rough, fast-paced business meant something—or so I thought. These were the folks in whom you confided about a tough deadline or your latest harried live shot from a gruesome crime scene or three-alarm fire. These were the ones who understood the pressure of broadcast news. I learned a lot of things in my years in news, including what the word "friendship" really meant. When my contract wasn't renewed and the news director sent me packing, the majority of these so-called friends were nowhere to be found.

Friends, Tried and True

So who were the last friends standing when the TV camera lights went out and when my common household name wasn't so common any longer? It was longtime friends such as Bridget and Lynn, both of whom you've read about already. Bridget knew me long before my face ever appeared on local television. Friends since our early teens, we were both Catholic, and in addition to being on the pompom squad, we also worked on the high school newspaper together. Despite going to different universities, we kept in close contact. Bridget got a kick out of seeing me on TV or hearing me on the radio. I was excited to see her grow her successful marketing career and go up against some of the big guns in the Motown ad agencies. But we never forgot where we came from, and we still do our best to keep each other grounded.

When Lynn and I met, because she was from an entirely different area of the country, she didn't have a clue as to who I was, media-wise. She found it interesting, but my high profile career really didn't matter. We hit it off on a much deeper level as sisters in Christ.

While both have been extremely supportive of my work, they also love me for who I am, not for what I do. And when I was struggling through unemployment, they were there to cheer me up, whether in person or on the phone. I've also tried to return the favor when they find themselves going through their own tough times. When Bridget was diagnosed with breast cancer, I was one of the first people she called. I prayed with her over the phone. We laughed and cried, and we even had a wig party at her house as she was trying to prepare for the effects of chemo. I can still remember sitting in her bathroom, each of us with a glass of wine in hand, trying on different wigs and laughing hysterically.

When Lynn, an experienced registered nurse, began contemplating leaving behind the hectic hospital life for a home-based position, she was a bit apprehensive at first. Since I had been working primarily from home for several years, I was able to answer a lot of her questions and serve as a sounding board.

While Bridget and Lynn are two of my oldest and closest friends, the Lord has blessed me with a long list of newer friends that my husband and I also cherish. When I began my ministry some sixteen years ago, little by little, wonderful people came into our lives. Some were there for a short period of time, while others are still companions on the journey. God brought them to us at the right time for just the right reason. Whether it was helping us grow in our knowledge of Scripture or helping me build a website and a speaking ministry, new acquaintances and special friends were made.

I also can't imagine my life without my dear friend Laurie. Dominick and I met Laurie and her husband, Rick, at a Christian conference nearly fifteen years ago. In addition to our annual Christmastime dinner at my house and dreamy excursions on their boat in the summertime, we try to get together as often as we can. Even if we can't see each other, there are always lots of meaningful e-mails and calls in between visits. Laurie is one of the truly most thoughtful and selfless women I know. And she has such a gift for making you feel special!

About ten years ago, my husband and I served as the cohosts of a Catholic couples' cruise to Turkey, following the footsteps of St. Paul. This was the second pilgrimage that I was involved in through Catholic radio. By this time, we were growing close to the owner of the Catholic travel agency, John, and his wife, Kristan. We quickly fell in love with their five adorable children, and that cruise sealed the deal. Now we can't imagine our lives without them and their children. Another couple on the cruise, Carol and Bill, are also part of our growing family of friends. They're our age, and Carol is a crazy Calabrese (from the southern part of Italy) like me. Most important, they love the Lord and the Church and are a heck of a lot of fun.

My work in Catholic media has helped to grow my list of companions in other ways. And even if they move away, the bond that is built on Christ keeps us close. I was heartbroken when my friend Mary told me that she and her husband were moving to Atlanta for her husband's business. I was happy for them in their new adventure, and also because Mary would be closer to her grandchildren, but sad for me and my husband, Dom—well, to be quite honest, mostly sad for me. Mary was a fellow broadcaster and had also worked in Catholic radio. She is one of those friends who really gets what I do on a daily basis. Thank goodness for Facebook, FaceTime, texting, and e-mails!

Then there are friends with whom you identify so closely that they seem more like blood relatives, or sisters, than friends. That's the case with Janet. When we met ten years ago, we discovered that we had much in common, including an estranged sibling that had caused a lot of pain in our lives. That common experience, plus our work in Catholic evangelization and the pro-life movement, cemented our friendship and sisterhood, to the point where we now finish each other's sentences.

I've heard it said, "Friends are God's way of taking care of us." I don't know who said it, but I know it's true. You can't "outgive" God. It seems the closer I get to the Lord, the more he blesses me, especially in the "friends" category. So if you're worried that your efforts to grow in your faith will mean the phone will stop ringing or your dance card, so to speak, won't be so full any longer, don't be. We serve an amazingly loving and generous God who has already given us ten thousand-plus heavenly pals. So it goes without saying, but I'll say it anyway: when it comes to providing companions for your journey here on earth, trust me, God will take care of you to the point where your friendship travel mug will be overflowing.

CHAPTER 11

Cast Out Your Nets

COMPANIONS *IN PERSONA CHRISTI*

*As he passed by the Sea of Galilee, he saw Simon and his
brother Andrew casting their nets into the sea; they were
fishermen. Jesus said to them, "Come after me,
and I will make you fishers of men."*

—Mark 1:16-17

We can't cast out our nets into this sea of life if those nets
are nothing more than tangled webs of pain, unforgiveness,
doubt, and anger. Oftentimes, however, that is exactly what
happens on this journey of faith. We want to keep moving
forward, growing closer to God. We want to dive deeper into
his mercy and follow his will for us, but we can't seem to
loosen the grip of the past. We're stuck standing by the boat,
trying to unravel all the emotional knots that have formed

in the nets of our hearts. And we can't serve Jesus very well as "fishers of men" if we can't get beyond the shore. While Jesus doesn't promise smooth sailing even when we do eventually venture out, he does provide safe harbors as well as faithful captains to help us stay on course. Thank God for holy priests who give their lives for Jesus and his Church.

Our priests often don't get the credit they deserve. Unfortunately, because of the gravely sinful behavior of a small percentage involved in the sexual-abuse scandal, a fair number of Catholics, even those not personally affected by the abuse, lost their faith in God and the Church and walked away. While the pope himself reminds us that the Church must continue to make efforts to repair that broken trust, we shouldn't let the sins of a few keep us from the sacraments administered through the priesthood, because those sacraments are truly the vehicles used by God to transmit his grace and love.

Our parish priests and pastors continually do so much with so little. After my husband was ordained to the diaconate in 2012, I could see the challenges religious face in a very up close and personal way. It always seems that a handful of parish volunteers are doing the majority of the work when it comes to assisting at various events like parish festivals, fish fries, catechism classes, Bible studies, and so forth. And yet it often seems that just about the only thing the rest of the congregation is good at is offering criticism to Fr. So-and-So, and much of it not at all constructive. In many ways, the priesthood can be a thankless job, even though we could not experience the fullness of our faith without our priests. They also accompany us and are there for us during the most important moments of our lives.

Priests are neither canonized saints nor girlfriends, but in my continued journey of faith and, more specifically, during my slow journey back to God, they have been companions who have helped me find my way home. Years ago, during one of my most powerful experiences of confession, it was a priest who helped me see how my inability to forgive myself was holding me back spiritually and emotionally. At the time, I didn't think I was still carrying all that much baggage. I knew that God had forgiven me for all of my selfishness and the obsession with my career that had led to a lot of the problems in my relationships and, in particular, in my marriage. Little did I know that I had not forgiven myself.

We had been back in the Church for only a short time but we knew the importance of confession, so Dominick and I headed to our church together. It was the week before Holy Week of 1994, and our parish had brought in additional priests from around the archdiocese to help hear confessions. Since we only had a handful of actual confessionals, several of the priests were stationed in different areas around the church. At the time, I had a habit of going to priests I didn't know. Maybe that was an outward sign of some of my inward baggage, but with my work in the secular media at that point, it just made it less embarrassing for me.

I don't know what I was expecting that day, probably the peace that comes from knowing that one has taken the time to once again repent and reflect. What I received was even greater than that. The priest had his eyes closed the entire time I was making my confession. After I was done, he opened his eyes and made absolutely no mention of the venial sins I had just mentioned. It wasn't that what I had confessed wasn't important. It was that God knew that I needed to hear an important message. This priest had the most intense blue eyes I have ever seen. He looked at me lovingly and very gently said something that shot right to my heart of hearts: "Why don't you yet see yourself as a beloved daughter of God?"

Although the priest was looking right at me, I knew it was Jesus speaking through him, acting in what the *Catechism* calls *in persona Christi* or "in the person of Christ."

In the ecclesial service of the ordained minister, it is Christ himself who is present to his Church as Head of his Body, Shepherd of his flock, high priest of the redemptive sacrifice, Teacher of Truth. This is what the Church means by saying that the priest, by virtue of the sacrament of Holy Orders, acts *in persona Christi Capitis*. (1548)

I don't remember much after that. The priest gave me my penance, and I went back to the pew and began to sob. What he said was so true. Deep in my soul, I knew I just didn't feel good enough to be loved, not only by my husband, but by God. I had ignored my family and faith for so long and had caused a lot of damage. Even after all the times I had gone to confession, it just hadn't sunk in—until that moment. Ironically, or maybe not so ironically, I had never seen that priest before, and in all my years of practicing my faith and getting to know most of the priests in the Archdiocese of Detroit by name, I never saw him again. But I never forgot him or that particular confession. It not only freed me from my self-loathing, but it also gave me an even greater respect for the Sacrament of Reconciliation.

God Revealing Himself

My friend Paula, whom I mentioned in the first chapter, had a similarly powerful experience during a session with her spiritual director as well as through a series of dreams that followed. Paula had been receiving direction from this priest for some time, and they were both trying to work through the emotional and spiritual fallout from some abuse she had suffered earlier in her life. As she explains, it was like that old saying "One step forward and two steps back." She would make progress but then get stuck again, not truly finding enough strength to let go and let God.

> When we first began meeting in 2009, I was at a very low point and extremely vulnerable. I was plagued by a very dark past and was desperately seeking to find the Light. Father had walked down many a dark road with me, and by January 2012, I guess we were both rather weary of the journey, which may have been, in part, what prompted the question that was completely out of character for him: "Does Mrs. Paula even want to be happy?"

According to Paula, the fact that it was a fair and legitimate question did nothing to reduce its sting. She was humiliated that he even considered the question, much less verbalized it.

Not too long after that particularly rough session, Paula had the first of three dreams. She found herself sitting inside the parlor of her parish rectory. Seated next to her was, as she describes, "Father but not Father": "It was his body. It was not his voice. Yet it was surely a voice I recognized, in the sense that I was certain I had heard it before, only I could not quite put a face or a name to its owner."

The happiness question came up again in that dream and two other similar dreams. Eventually, the dreams helped Paula realize that she was wrapped tightly in a web of emotional baggage. She had been getting herself caught up in thread after thread of self-doubt, not forgiving herself and continuing to blame herself for the wrong done to her—something out of her control but for which she still felt responsible. The emotional turmoil was causing distress in her own life and having a negative impact on her marriage and family. The dreams, with clear imagery of a net being loosened and cast off, eventually helped her to move well beyond the pain and give herself fully to God, her husband, and her family. She believes that the body in the chair that looked like her spiritual director but wasn't and the voice that she had heard before both belonged to Jesus.

A few weeks later, Paula went to adoration before Mass, asking Jesus if what she had experienced in the dreams was real.

The Mass began, and the deacon approached the pulpit to proclaim Mark's Gospel. Imagine my heart skipping a beat when I heard him proclaim, "'This is the time of fulfillment. The kingdom of God is at hand. Repent, and believe in the gospel.' As he passed by the Sea of Galilee, he saw Simon and his brother Andrew casting their nets into the sea; they were fishermen. Jesus said to them, 'Come after me, and I will make you fishers of men.' Then they abandoned their nets and followed him." (Mark 1:15-18)

At various times in both the Old and New Testaments, dreams were used as a means of communicating urgent messages. St. Joseph was told the truth about Jesus' paternity in a dream and was also warned in a dream to flee to Egypt (see Matthew 1:18-24; 2:13-15). And the Old Testament prophet Joel tells us that God can speak to us in dreams as well: "It will come to pass / I will pour out my spirit upon all flesh. / Your sons and daughters will prophesy, / your old men will dream dreams, / your young men will see visions" (3:1).

Paula received additional affirmation from her spiritual director after consulting with him about her experiences.

After I wrote of my encounter with Jesus in my dreams and had the occasion to read it to him, both of us were stricken with tears and the belief that something "holy" had happened. Oddly, the dream was also a confirmation for him of his call to the priesthood and assurance that he was right where God wants him to be. It was also proof to him that God does reveal himself *in persona Christi* through the priest. Perhaps the dream has become as significant for him as it is for me.

St. Paul tells us in 1 Timothy 2:4 that he desires all men to be saved. Because of that desire for not one of his sheep to be lost, Jesus is constantly conducting a major search and rescue mission, using a variety of means to bring us back into the fold. We see how he works through the saints in heaven, his children on earth, his word, and, at times, even in dreams. Surely the High Priest who instituted the Sacrament of Holy Orders himself would want us to consider his shepherds as companions for our faith journey as well.

Conclusion

YOU'RE RIGHT WHERE YOU NEED TO BE

May you trust God that you are exactly
where you are meant to be.
—From a prayer attributed to St. Teresa of Avila

I will wrap up this book the same way I started: with one more powerful story about how the Lord speaks through his saints. I mention these dramatic examples from St. Teresa of Avila and now St. Gabriel in hopes that you will understand that God is waiting to reveal his love in eye-opening ways to everyone. Maybe I need more help than most people. Maybe because of my thick, stubborn Italian head, or "testa dura" as my *paisanos* would say, I need quite a few houses to fall on me—or holy two-by-fours upside the head—to keep me focused. I need the spotlights and the bright neon signs dropping down in front of me, reminding me that God is still very large and very much in charge. My St. Gabriel encounter is like something right out of a Frank Capra feel-good film.

It was early November in 2004, and I could not wait to get to Mass. I had only been in Catholic radio for about two years at that point, but already I was feeling like I didn't belong. The presidential election was over, but when it came to my coverage of the event, I felt like I had been in the middle of a boxing ring for the last several days instead of sitting behind a microphone. As hard as I tried to be balanced and informative, I just couldn't seem to please anyone.

While we're not allowed to endorse candidates on Catholic radio, just as in the Church, we are called to help the faithful, and in my case, radio listeners, understand the issues from a Catholic perspective. That means we bring on theologians, cultural analysts, and experts on the various issues on the ballot. We also examine Church teaching as it pertains to the platforms of those running for office and their parties.

"Our Catholic faith shouldn't be a factor when we go to the polls but *the* factor," I would often say when leading into an election-related segment. It was a quote from a great homily I had heard a few weeks before the election that year. In other words, we don't leave our faith behind when we cast our ballots. Our faith is supposed to mean something beyond our Sunday obligations.

Even though I never mentioned any names, those who supported George Bush thought I was rooting for John Kerry, and vice versa. I was too liberal for the Republicans in the audience and too conservative for the Democrats. It was not a pretty picture, and neither was the flood of e-mails and other negative feedback the station was receiving. Management was very supportive, as the staff had been closely working together to make sure we were covering the elections from a truly Catholic and nonpartisan perspective. We knew that no matter what, some would find fault with our efforts.

Yet I found the entire experience very unsettling and confusing. This wasn't what I had expected from the audience, especially Catholic listeners. I really thought, given the faith factor along with my own professional reputation, that they wouldn't be so harsh. And so I examined myself. "Maybe I wasn't as prepared as I should have been going into the interviews. Maybe I am not as 'fair and balanced' as I thought. Is Catholic radio where I'm supposed to be?"

These were just a few of the questions I kept asking myself as I sat during Mass the Sunday following the 2004 elections. Certainly it wasn't about hurt feelings. Having been in the media my entire professional life, I had developed a thick skin. This was something more: again, a questioning about what people wanted or expected from Catholic radio and Catholic radio hosts. Perhaps a Catholic who was trained as a secular reporter wasn't the right fit.

I had shared my concerns with my husband, who lovingly advised me to take it to prayer during Mass. So I did just that, even offering up Communion for whatever God wanted. I also asked that if he still wanted me in Catholic media, he would give me some sort of a sign—even just a hint of some sort—that I was where I was supposed to be. "If this new radio gig was a temporary stop along the path you have planned, I am fine with that, God, but please point me in the right direction," I pleaded as I walked up to receive Communion.

I felt a little bit better as we walked out of Mass and headed for the car. Everything was in God's hands. He had always taken care of me before, so I had no doubt that he would come through again. I had forgotten, however, how quickly he sometimes answers our prayers.

We were just about to pull out of the parish parking lot when we saw one of the ushers, Bob, running up to our car. He tapped urgently on the window.

"Teresa, I haven't seen you in a few weeks, but I have been looking for you. I have had this for over a month. A woman came up to me and told me to give this to you if I saw you. I don't know her name, but she wanted to make sure I passed this on," he said, almost out of breath.

He handed me the item through the window, and Dominick and I both gasped. It was a medal of St. Gabriel, the patron saint of communications workers. Gabriel is one of the most important saints for those working in the media because of his announcement, or "annunciation," to Mary regarding the birth of Jesus.

In the center of the circular medal is an image of St. Gabriel blowing his trumpet. He is surrounded by images representing communications, including, of course, a TV and a radio. Circling the outer rim of the medal are the words "Patron of Communications, Radio, and TV."

"Honey, I think you have your answer as to where God wants you to be," my husband said as I started to cry.

I should have known something was up when Bob said he didn't recognize the woman who had approached him. Bob has been an usher for years. He's very friendly and makes it a point to greet and meet as many people in the parish as possible. Maybe the woman just happened to be passing through and stopped at our church. Maybe she was a new parishioner that Bob hadn't bumped into yet. Whatever the case, God made sure that all the pieces fell into place so that I would receive the medal just when I needed it most—not a week or two earlier, but right after I had asked him to show me the way.

So if you take away just one message from this book, I hope it's this: that the saints are there for you. There are one or more of them with whom you can identify, a saint that understands your personality as well as your plight. Let's do our best to embrace the saints, both in heaven and on earth, all the holy men and women that God puts in our path to help us enjoy this life as we travel to our final destination.

Last but not least, take another look around right now and remember that this is exactly where you're meant to be. Remember too that you are not alone. With every step, just keep moving toward Christ and his Church, and be sure to invite a few girlfriends and other saints along for the journey.

ENDNOTES

1. C. S. Lewis, *The Four Loves* (San Diego: Harcourt Brace Jovanovich, 1960), 113.

2. Augustine, *Confessions* (London: Penguin Books, 1961), 231-232.

3. "Meditation: Numbers 11:14–15," *The Word Among Us,* August 2015, http://wau.org/meditations/2015/08/03.

4. Ibid.

5. Mark Shea, "Saints: Our Unseen Prayer Partners," *National Catholic Register,* July 5, 2015, http://www.ncregister.com/blog/mark-shea/saints-our-unseen-prayer-partners.

6. Augustine, 169.

7. Benedict XVI, General Audience, October 13, 2010, https://w2.vatican.va/content/benedict-xvi/en/audiences/2010/documents/hf_ben-xvi_aud_20101013.html.

8. Ibid.

9. John Paul II, Homily on a Pastoral Visit to the Argentine National Church in Rome, November 13, 1998, §4, http://w2.vatican.va/content/john-paul-ii/en/homilies/1998/documents/hf_jp-ii_hom_19981113_argentina.html.

10. John Paul II, Address to the Communications Staff, October 2, 1979, https://w2.vatican.va/content/john-paul-ii/en/speeches/1979/october/documents/hf_jp-ii_spe_19791002_usa-social-comm.pdf.

11. John Paul II, Homily for the Inauguration Mass of his Pontificate, October 22, 1978, §5, https://w2.vatican.va/content/john-paul-ii/en/homilies/1978/documents/hf_jp-ii_hom_19781022_inizio-pontificato.html.

12. John Paul II, *Salvifici Doloris* (On the Christian Meaning of Human Suffering), §14, http://w2.vatican.va/content/john-paul-ii/en/apost_letters/1984/documents/hf_jp-ii_apl_11021984_salvifici-doloris.html.

13. Ibid., §25.

14. Teresa of Avila, "In the Hands of God," *The Collected Works of St. Teresa of Avila*, vol. III, trans. Kieran Kavanaugh, OCD, and Otilio Rodriguez, OCD (ICS Publications: Washington, DC, 1985), 377.

15. Ibid., 377–378.

16. Ibid., 379.

17. Paul Hamans, *Edith Stein and Companions: On the Way to Auschwitz* (San Francisco: Ignatius Press, 2010), p. 87.

18. John Paul II, *Evangelium Vitae* (The Gospel of Life), March 25, 1995, §99, http://w2.vatican.va/content/john-paul-ii/en/encyclicals/documents/hf_jp-ii_enc_25031995_evangelium-vitae.html.

19. Edith Stein, "The Ethos of Women's Professions," *Essays on Woman (The Collected Works of Edith Stein)*, 2nd ed., rev., eds. Lucy Gelber and Romaeus Leuven, OCD, trans. Freda Mary Oben (ICS Publications: Washington, DC, 1996).

theWORD among us®
The *Spirit* of Catholic Living

This book was published by The Word Among Us. Since 1981, The Word Among Us has been answering the call of the Second Vatican Council to help Catholic laypeople encounter Christ in the Scriptures.

The name of our company comes from the prologue to the Gospel of John and reflects the vision and purpose of all of our publications: to be an instrument of the Spirit, whose desire is to manifest Jesus' presence in and to the children of God. In this way, we hope to contribute to the Church's ongoing mission of proclaiming the gospel to the world so that all people would know the love and mercy of our Lord and grow more deeply in their faith as missionary disciples.

Our monthly devotional magazine, *The Word Among Us*, features meditations on the daily and Sunday Mass readings, and currently reaches more than one million Catholics in North America and another half million Catholics in one hundred countries around the world. Our book division, The Word Among Us Press, publishes numerous books, Bible studies, and pamphlets that help Catholics grow in their faith.

To learn more about who we are and what we publish, log on to our website at www.wau.org. There you will find a variety of Catholic resources that will help you grow in your faith.

Embrace His Word, Listen to God . . .